DESKTOP PUBLIS
SOURCEBOOK

FONTS
and
CLIP-ART

For the
Macintosh™

Jami Lynne Borman

UK Edition

A Kuma/Prima Publication

Kuma Computers Ltd.,
12 Horseshoe Park,
Pangbourne,
Berks RG8 7JW
0734 844335 TEL
0734 844339 FAX

Editing, Typography, and Production by Instruction Writers.
Jacket Design by Wolfe Design Group.

Prima Publishing & Communications
Rocklin, CA

ISBN 0-7457-0050-0

First USA edition published by:-

Prima Publishing & Communications
P.O. Box 1260MAC
Rocklin,
CA 95677
USA
916 624 5718 TEL

First UK edition published by:-

Kuma Computers Ltd.,
12 Horseshoe Park,
Pangbourne,
Berks RG8 7JW
UK
0734 844335 TEL
0734 844339 FAX

Dedication

This book is dedicated to Thomas M. Schach, whose relentless efforts and unselfish dedication of time and energy made this book possible.

Acknowledgements

My many thanks to the following writers and artists for their contribution in preparing this manuscript: Gene Bjerke, Scott Borman-Allen, Cyrus Creveling, Edward Offutt, Thomas M. Schach, C. Claire Smith, and Chris Van Buren.

I would also like to thank the companies represented in this book for their contribution of time, technical assistance, and evaluation software.

Thanks to all of you at St. Martin's Press, Prima Publishing, Bookman Productions, Waterside Productions, and Washington Apple Pi for your input and enthusiastic support of this project. And especially to Ben Dominitz who helped make my idea for this book a reality.

STOP PRESS

Great effort has gone in to validating all the sourcing information. If the reader experiences difficulty please contact Tim Moore at Kuma Computers Ltd for the latest information (as there are often secondary sources within the UK). For future editions of the Sourcebook, originators of Fonts & Clip-Art packages are invited to make contact and furnish information about their products.

Contents

3   PostScript Fonts

4   Font Companies

5   Working With Graphics

6 Graphic Companies

7 Appendix

1 Introduction

Welcome to *Desktop Publishing Sourcebook (Red Book, for short)* for the Macintosh. If you're an experienced desktop publisher (or even if you're not) you'll find this book indispensable. No need to drive for hours or read through mountains of brochures to find what you need. The *Red Book* brings the store to you.

Throughout these pages you'll find hundreds of font and clip-art (graphic) samples from dozens of manufacturers. We've even included two chapters which cover font and graphic basics. Learning the basics will help make your font and graphic purchases go more smoothly. (See Chapter 2, *Working With Fonts* and Chapter 5, *Working With Graphics*.)

How This Book Can Help You

The *Red Book* shows you so many fonts and graphics that it's hard to spend much time with the book without getting your creative juices flowing.

But the main goal of the *Red Book* is to help you quickly put your fingers on the information you need. It tells you the *who*, the *what*, and the *what else* of fonts and graphics.

The Who

The *Who*, of course, are the companies who make fonts and graphics. Suppose that you want to know...

Which company carries a font that you like.

Look-up the font alphabetically in Chapter 3, *PostScript Fonts*, and you'll find out.

How to contact a font or graphic company.

Check the company's listing in Chapter 4, *Font Companies* or Chapter 6, *Graphic Companies*. Here you'll find a short profile about each company and their products as well as the company's address, phone number, and FAX number.

Which companies make a specific foreign language or symbol font.

In the *Appendix*, you'll find two alphabetical listings: one for foreign language fonts and another for symbol fonts. Each foreign language and symbol font is accompanied by the names of the companies which offer the font. At the end of the *Appendix*, each company's name, address, and phone number is listed.

The What

The *What* refers to the fonts and graphics themselves. Suppose you want to...

Learn some fonts basics.

Read Chapter 2, *Working With Fonts*. This chapter has information on how to use, print, and refer to fonts.

Learn more about graphics.

Open the book to Chapter 5, *Working With Graphics*. Here you'll learn about graphic formats, the differences between paint programs and draw programs, and how to scale a graphic image while keeping it in proportion.

See hundreds of font samples.

Open the *Red Book* to Chapter 3, *PostScript Fonts*. Here you'll find hundreds of font samples in alphabetical order, each displayed in 14pt type.

Each sample includes the entire upper and lower case alphabet[1], the numbers 0-9, and several popular symbols. The companies that carry the font follow each font sample.

See hundreds of clip-art samples.

Turn to Chapter 6, *Graphic Companies*. Here you'll find sample clip-art from each collection that each graphic company offers.[2] You can also read about each company and its product line.

Know which font package includes the font you've selected.

Chapter 4, *Font Companies*, displays see each company's product line of English-language fonts organized by font package. (Most fonts are sold in *families* that include three or four weights of the same font style.) You can find a font by browsing through the package listings or looking-up the font name in the *Index*.

What foreign language fonts and symbol fonts are available for the Mac.

In the *Appendix* you'll discover a list of foreign language fonts and a list of symbol fonts. Each font is followed by the name of the companies which offer it.

---

[1] Some display fonts do not include lower case letters.

[2] *Archive Arts* only provided the author with two complete clip-art packages. For this reason, only two of their packages are shown.

The What Else

Some products are also available for the IBM.

If your office uses both Macs and IBMs, you may want to purchase identical fonts or graphics for both systems.

In Chapter 3 *(Font Companies)* and Chapter 6 *(Graphic Companies)* you'll find a key in the upper right-hand corner of the first page of each company's listing. This key tells you whether the company's products are only available for the Macintosh, or are also available for the IBM.

When the key indicates that IBM-compatible products are available, it doesn't necessarily mean that *all* of the company's products are available in the IBM format. Read the short section of text that follows the company listing to determine what part of the product line is available for IBM-compatible computers.

For a broader selection of fonts and graphics for the IBM PC and compatibles, see Jami Lynne Borman's *Desktop Publishing Sourcebook, Fonts and Clip-Art For the IBM PC and Compatibles* (Prima Publishing).

What You See Is How It Looks.

All of the text and samples for the *Red Book* were produced using 300 dpi (dots per inch) laser printers. Why didn't we use a typesetter (1000⁺ dpi)? Because most businesses are using 300 dpi laser printers to produce their final copy.

Since most of our readers are printing at 300 dpi, we elected to show the font and graphic samples at the same resolution as most office laser printers. Of course, if you are using a typesetter, your output will look even better than the samples in this book.

Take advantage of the *Red Book*'s cross-referencing.

When you see a font in Chapter 3 *(PostScript Fonts)* that you'd like to purchase, check the names of the font companies that offer the font.

Next, flip to Chapter 4 *(Font Companies)* to locate a company that offers the font. Browse through the pages that follow the company listing to identify which font package includes the font you selected. Alternatively, you can look-up the font name in the *Index*.

Purchasing fonts and clip-art.

Many of the fonts and graphics displayed on these pages *cannot* be found at your local software store. Fortunately, most font and graphics companies will sell you their products directly or at least point you to a store that carries them.

Upon request, *some* companies will also sell a font or graphic individually--although the per item price will not be as competitive at the package price. If you prefer to purchase an individual font or graphic instead of the entire package, just contact the company and ask them.

Printers and the Mac

Three types of printers are commonly used when desktop publishing on a Mac. They are listed below in the order of best to worst print quality. Not so coincidentally, this list is also in order of most to least expensive.

- PostScript Laser Printers

- Non-PostScript Laser Printers

- Dot Matrix Printers

The *resolution* (print quality) of a laser printer is measured in dots per linear inch, commonly referred to as *dpi*. The higher the dpi, the sharper the printed image. Typeset quality begins around 1000 dpi.

Most business use laser printers, rather than dot matrix printers, because of their superior print quality. Laser printers for the Mac typically have a resolution of 300 dpi (90,000 dots per square inch) compared to 72 dpi for dot matrix printers.

Over the next year or so, you'll see changes to this 300 dpi standard as affordable printers are introduced to the market with resolutions of 400 dpi and up. (Printers are discussed in more detail in Chapter 2, *Working With Fonts.*)

How Does Postscript Work?

PostScript is a page description language licensed by Adobe Systems, Inc. PostScript instructions are sent to the printer by the Mac. The Mac describes the shape of each PostScript character or graphic to be printed. The printer, upon receiving these instructions, converts each object into a dot pattern. The dot patterns are then fused to your paper using *toner,* an ink-like chemical.

PostScript Laser Printers

PostScript laser printers have a processor (a brain) which converts the PostScript instructions (sent by your computer) into the dots that make up the printed image. This processor is what make PostScript laser printers more expensive than non-Postscript laser printers. Not all PostScript printers use the Abode-licensed language. Printers which do not use Adobe PostScript are considered *PostScript-compatible* printers.

Non-PostScript Laser Printers

Non-PostScript laser printers are less expensive than their PostScript cousins. They vary in features, typically have 300 dpi resolution, and sport a limited number of high-quality fonts. They do *not*, however, understand PostScript language instructions.

Dot Matrix Printers

Dot matrix printers can reproduce any fonts and graphics that are displayed on your screen (including PostScript fonts). But this credit belongs to the Macintosh--not to the printer. The Mac tells the dot matrix printer to print a specific series of dots each time the *print head* passes over the paper. These dots form a picture of the screen or the information on the screen.

Because of their generally low print-quality when compared to laser printers, dot matrix printers are rarely used by businesses for producing final output. They can, however, be a valuable tool for making *proofing* (test) copies before printing your final copy on the laser printer.

Getting Included

If your company produces original fonts or clip art and would like to be included in the next edition of the *Red Book*, please contact the author at the address shown below.

About The Author

Jami Lynne Borman is Director of Software Support for Instruction Writers, a company in Gaithersburg, Maryland which writes user manuals for computer software.

Ms. Borman's other books include

Desktop Publishing Sourcebook Fonts and Clip-Art For the IBM PC and Compatibles (Prima Publishing)

WordPerfect 5 Desktop Publishing Ideas & Techniques (COMPUTE! Books)

WordPerfect Business Macros (Scott Foresman).

Getting In Touch

The author would like to receive your comments on how future editions of the *Red Book* can be improved. You may write to her (no phone calls please) care of

Instruction Writers
P.O. Box 2218
Montgomery Village, Maryland 20886

Working With Fonts

The Macintosh has become a serious desktop publishing tool for business and industry. Deciding to buy your Mac was easy; deciding which fonts to buy for the Mac can be very complicated.

If you are just beginning to work with fonts (or have never worked with them before), you need to learn some basic terms that are commonly used in desktop publishing (e.g., *point size*, *font style*, and *leading*).

Once you understand font terminology, you're ready to learn how the Macintosh uses fonts. You'll discover the Mac's font limitations, how to add fonts to your system, and how the Mac and your printer work together. By the end of this chapter, you'll be ready to make informed decisions about selecting, using, and purchasing fonts.

Font Basics

What Is A Font?

A font is a collection of characters (called a character set) of the same size and type style. Most character sets include at minimum the characters shown on the following page.

Upper Case Alphabet
    ABCDEFGHIJKLMNOPQRSTUVWXYZ
Lower Case Alphabet
    abcdefghijklmnopqrstuvwxyz
Numbers
    1234567890
Punctuation marks
    !,.?;:'"
Popular Symbols
    <>/[]{}=+-_()*&^%$#@~'\ |

Many character sets also include bullets, arrows, foreign language accents, the copyright mark, the line draw characters, and other useful symbols.[1]

Talking About Fonts

Every font is identified by its *style, weight* and *size*.

Times Roman	**Bold**	**16pt**
ITC Bookman	Light	10pt
Helvetica Narrow	*Oblique*	*14pt*

You don't need the italic or bold versions of a font to display *italics* or **boldface** on your screen. You do, however, need those versions to print italics or boldface on your PostScript printer.

Font Style

The font style is the *look* of the font--the characteristics that make it visually unique. Every font is referred to by its style

---

[1] Some special purpose fonts (e.g., dingbats, display fonts) may not include all the characters in a typical character set.

name. For example,

> Times Roman
> Helvetica
> Palatino
> New Century Schoolbook
> Avant Garde

Many style names have the name of the type foundry (the company that designed the font) as a prefix. The two most common prefixes are *CG* (Compugraphic Corporation) and *ITC* (International Typeface Corporation).

Font Size

Font size is measured in points (pts). The size most often used for text is 10-12 pts. Point size is a vertical measurement; horizontal measurement is not taken into consideration. At first, you may find it awkward to use a measurement with which you are unfamiliar; but soon it will feel very natural to refer to a font in points. *(See Figure 2.1.)*

A point is equivalent to 1/72 inch--the same as a picture element on your Macintosh screen. As you install fonts into your System file, notice the many different point sizes that are available.

When measuring a font's point size, the measurement is taken from the top of an ascender (b, f, h, k, l, t) to the bottom of a descender (g, j, p, q, y). Since few characters have both an ascender and a descender, an individual character typically does not measure the full point size. Letters in different font styles can have different vertical measurements--even when the letters are the same point size. *(See Figure 2.2.)*

A font's *x-height* refers to the size of a character, ignoring its ascender and/or descender. X-height also refers to the size of a font's characters that have no ascender or descender (a, c, e, m, n, o, r, s, u, v, w, x, z).

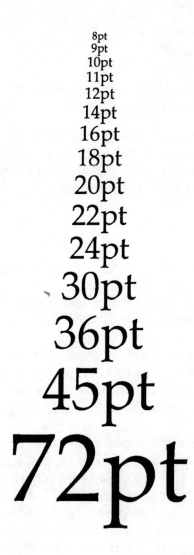

8pt
9pt
10pt
11pt
12pt
14pt
16pt
18pt
20pt
22pt
24pt
30pt
36pt
45pt
72pt

Figure 2.1

X-HEIGHT

xylophone   xylophone

Avant Garde 20pt   Times Roman 20pt

Figure 2.2

Did you know that many programs let you use point sizes that aren't even installed in your system? They do, as long as you have installed at least *one* size of the font style you select.

How does this work? Before the Macintosh displays a font on your screen, it looks in the System file for the font name and size you requested. If the Mac finds the font, it uses it. If the Mac doesn't find the font, it creates the size you requested by scaling another font of the same style.

For example, suppose you have installed 12pt Park Avenue but not 18pt Park Avenue. When you ask the Mac for 18pt Park Avenue, it *scales* the 12pt font to 18pt--the result of which can be less than attractive. When you use a dot matrix printer, your printout looks similar to the screen image.

PostScript printers, however, are better at scaling fonts than the Macintosh. When you scale PostScript fonts and print them on a PostScript printer, your pages printout beautifully, although the fonts still look unattractive on the screen.

Font Weight

Weight refers to the heft and/or slant of a font. Most fonts are available in the four weights shown below.

> Medium (or Roman or Book)
> **Bold**
> *Italics (or Oblique)*
> ***Bold Italics (or Bold Oblique)***

Some decorative fonts (e.g., *Zapf Chancery® Medium Italic*) are only available in one weight. A few fonts (e.g., Helvetica) are available in many more weights than the four listed above. (See Chapter 3, *PostScript Fonts*.)

Letter Spacing

Most fonts are *proportionally* spaced. In other words, the amount of horizontal space that is used by each letter varies, depending on the letter. For example, an *m* takes up more line space than an *i* or a *j*.

Some fonts are *fixed-pitch*. Fixed-pitch fonts are similar to typewriter type in that each letter occupies the same amount of line space. Fixed-pitch fonts are typically measured in characters per inch (cpi). Most printers come with at least one fixed-pitch font, usually courier, built-in.

Courier Sample (fixed-pitch)

```
Who are you who lives behind my mirror?
You follow my every move.  Are you
imitating me or am I imitating you?
```

Times Roman Sample (proportionally spaced)

Who are you who lives behind my mirror? You follow my every move. Are you imitating me or am I imitating you?

Kerning

Kerning is a type of letter spacing between specific letter pairs (e.g., *th* and *fi*). The space between the letters is reduced to improve their aesthetics and readability. Kerning is not very visible in fonts smaller than 16 points.

Most word processing and page layout programs allow you, at minimum, to turn kerning on and off. Other programs

14

let you control which letter pairs are kerned and how close together the letters are placed.

Line Spacing

Many word processing and page layout programs allow you to vary the amount of space between your lines of text. This space is called *leading* (rhymes with wedding). Font styles which have long ascenders or descenders need more leading than fonts that don't. In publishing, the font size and leading is described as a fraction. For example, *10/12* (which is read "10 on 12") indicates 10pt type with 2pt leading.

Unlike fonts, lines have a horizontal as well as a vertical measurement. This measurement is expressed in picas.

> 12pt = 1 pica
> 72pt = 1 inch
> 6 picas = 1 inch

Although many programs do not use the terms *leading* and *pica*, you should be familiar with them if you plan to have your documents typeset at the printer.

Font Groups

The type styles that you select for your document or presentation material effect how your message is perceived. This happens because fonts help to convey certain *feelings*. There is much discussion on the emotional effect that one type style has over another.

Fonts are not divided into classifications based on their emotional effect, but they are typically divided into three groups: Serif, Sans Serif, and Display.

Serif Fonts

Type styles in the *serif* group have additional strokes (serifs) at the bottom of each letter. These serifs are often referred to as *feet*. Serif type styles are typically considered businesslike, formal, and authoritative. Sample serif fonts include

> Courier
> Bookman
> Palatino
> Times Roman

Many people feel that serif type styles are more readable than sans-serif type styles for large bodies of text that are printed in 12pt type or smaller.

Sans Serif Fonts

Type styles in the *sans serif* group do not have serifs. As a matter of fact, *sans* means *without* in French. Sans serif fonts have very clean lines and are typically considered friendly, casual, and familiar. Sample sans serif fonts include

> Helvetica
> Avant Garde

Display Fonts

Display (or decorative) type styles can be either serif or sans serif. Type styles in this group are used when you want to create a dramatic effect in headings, logos, and product names. They are rarely used in long passages of text since they are typically difficult to read. Sample display fonts include

Broadway

Dom Casual

Park Avenue

Zapf Chancery Medium Italic

How the Macintosh Uses Fonts

Screen and Printer Fonts

The Macintosh uses two types of fonts: screen fonts and PostScript printer fonts. PostScript printer fonts are only used when printing on a PostScript printer; screen fonts are required by all Macintosh programs. Screen fonts are used to

- Display text on the screen.

- Print fonts on a non-PostScript printer.

Screen fonts are also called *bit-mapped* fonts because each letter is composed of a series of small dots (bits) that create a *map* of the character. *(See Figure 2.3.)*

All the characters on the Macintosh screen are displayed using a pattern of dots. There are 72 dots in each inch of the screen. This gives the Mac screen a resolution of 72 dpi (dots per inch).

When you install a font in your System file, you are providing the Mac with font descriptions (or patterns). These descriptions tell the Mac how to combine the dots on your screen to form the various characters.

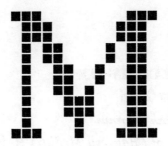

Figure 2.3

Screen fonts and printer fonts are related. When you go to print, the Mac *connects* each PostScript printer font to its corresponding screen font. Printer fonts have the instructions that your PostScript printer needs to produce high quality output.

Font Files

All fonts are stored in files. A font file (also called a *font suitcase*) can contain up to 500 fonts. Each point size in each type style is considered a separate font.

You can have several suitcases, depending on the amount of hard disk space you have on your computer. The *Font\DA Mover* utility that comes with the Mac is used to control which fonts are packed in which suitcase. For convenience, you may want to keep like type styles in the same suitcase.

Installing Fonts

Your word processing and other programs do not look in your suitcase files for fonts. You need to *install* the fonts in your System file using *Font\DA Mover*. Several of fonts are already installed in the System file; additional fonts can be found in a suitcase file on one of the Mac system disks.

When you first start *Font\DA Mover*, the left side of the screen shows you the fonts that are currently in the System file of the startup disk. *(The startup disk is the disk you used to start your computer--typically the hard disk.)*

To add fonts,

1. Click on *Open*.

   This presents a list box for selecting a suitcase file.

2. Select a suitcase file using the list box. (You can also select the System file from a different disk.)

   After choosing a suitcase, fonts appear in the right-hand box.

3. Highlight the fonts (the right side) that you want to copy to the System file (the left side). To select more than one font at a time, press [Shift] while clicking.

4. Click on *Copy*.

5. When finished, click on *Quit*.

   Mac copies the fonts you selected to the System file. All fonts in the System file appear automatically when you select fonts from any program.

Important: Never change the name of a printer font. The Mac links screen fonts to printer fonts by name.

Bold and Italic Fonts

In addition to the normal weight, most font styles are also available in **bold** and *italic*. When you activate these weights from within a program, the Mac displays bolded or italicized text on your screen.

Because you see bold and italics on your screen, you may be led to believe that you have installed these weights in your System file when, in fact, you haven't. It is recommended that you install the bold and italic weights for each type style in your System file.

Printing With Fonts

The Mac handles fonts differently depending on whether you are printing to a dot matrix printer, a non-PostScript laser printer, or a PostScript printer.

But before you can print on any of these devices, you must have installed screen fonts (in at least one point size) for every type style you plan to use. *(See **Installing Fonts**, above.)*

Dot Matrix Printers

When printing to a dot matrix printer, your screen font doubles as your printer font. If you can see it on your screen, you can print it on your printer. The drawback of dot matrix printers is their poor print quality; it is rarely better than your screen resolution of 72 dpi. For desktop publishing, dot matrix printers are best used for making draft printouts.

Non-PostScript Laser Printers

These printers come with several printer fonts built-in. When you go to print, the built-in fonts, whenever possible, are substituted for the fonts that were selected within your program. When a built-in font can not be substituted for the font on your screen, your printer reproduces the screen fonts, at a resolution similar to that of dot matrix printers.

Non-PostScript printers are a good choice when you

- Need a less-expensive alternative to PostScript.

- Do *not* need unlimited font capability.

- Desire the 300 dpi print-resolution that is commonly offered by the PostScript printers.

PostScript Laser Printers

Unlike the other printers, PostScript printers require *both* a screen font and a printer font. When you purchase a PostScript font, it comes with two sets of files: one for the screen and one for the printer. PostScript fonts may be used on dot matrix and non-PostScript laser printers, but in those cases you only need to use the screen font.

The advantages of using a PostScript printer include the printer's

- High-quality 300+ dpi output.

- Ability to scale PostScript fonts and graphics to any size without sacrificing print quality.

Downloading Fonts

Downloading is the process of sending font-information files to the printer. These files are placed in the printer's memory for use by your software programs. The fonts stay in the printer's memory until you turn off your printer or intentionally remove them. The downloading itself is performed using a utility program. Sometimes the utility is included when you buy a font package; other times it must be purchased separately.

Why bother downloading? When the printer comes across a font change in your document, it first looks to see if the font is one of its own built-in fonts. If not, the printer then determines whether or not the font has been downloaded to its memory. Lastly, if the printer is still unable to find the font, it checks the System file.

The advantage to downloading fonts is that the printer does not have to access the System file each time it encounters a font change. This saves time and allows your documents to be printed more quickly.

3 PostScript Fonts

There is no shortage to the selection of fonts that are available for your PostScript® printer. This chapter includes several hundred English-language font styles from

> Adobe® Systems, Inc.
> Agfa Corporation
> Alphabets, Inc.
> Dubl-Click Software, Inc.
> EmDash™
> Studio 231
> T/Maker Company

Each font is displayed in 14-point type and includes the name of the font; the upper and lower case alphabets; the numbers 0-9; and several symbols. Some fonts (such as those used for display) do not include all these characters. The fonts are listed in alphabetical order by font name, except when

- The font style is not the first part of the font name. For example, *Stempel Garamond* appears with the *Garamond* styles.

- The font name has a prefix such as *CG*, *ITC*, or *S*.

Below each font you'll find the company or companies that offer the font for sale. For more information about each font company and its product line, see Chapter 4, *Font Companies*.

Aachen Bold
ABCDEFGHIJKLMNOPQRSTUVWXYZ
abcdefghijklmnopqrstuvwxyz
1234567890?!$%&
Adobe Systems, Inc.

SAbbott Oldstyle
ABCDEFGHIJKLMNOPQRSTUVWXY
Zabcdefghijklmnopqrstuvwxyz
1234567890?!$%&
Studio 231

SACCANT
ABCDEFGHIJKLMNOPQRSTUVWXY
Z1234567890?!$%&
Studio 231

SAdlibs
ABCDEFGHIJKLMNOPQRSTUVWXYZ
abcdefghijklmnopqrstuvwxyz
1234567890?!$%&
Studio 231

Akzidenz Grotesk Roman
ABCDEFGHIJKLMNOPQRSTUVWXYZ
abcdefghijklmnopqrstuvwxyz
1234567890?!$%&
Adobe Systems, Inc.

Akzidenz Grotesk Bold
ABCDEFGHIJKLMNOPQRSTUVWXYZ
abcdefghijklmnopqrstuvwxyz
1234567890?!$%&
Adobe Systems, Inc.

Akzidenz Grotesk® Black
ABCDEFGHIJKLMNOPQRSTUVWXYZ
abcdefghijklmnopqrstuvwxyz
1234567890?!$%&
Adobe Systems, Inc.

Akzidenz Grotesk Light
ABCDEFGHIJKLMNOPQRSTUVWXYZ
abcdefghijklmnopqrstuvwxyz
1234567890?!$%&
Adobe Systems, Inc.

SAlbertus
ABCDEFGHIJKLMNOPQRSTUVWXYZ
abcdefghijklmnopqrstuvwxyz
1234567890?!$%&
Studio 231

SALBERTUS BLACK
ABCDEFGHIJKLMNOPQRSTUVWXYZ
1234567890?!$%&
Studio 231

SAlbertus Inline
ABCDEFGHIJKLMNOPQRSTUVWXYZ
abcdefghijklmnopqrstuvwxyz
1234567890?!$%&
Studio 231

SAlbertus Outline
ABCDEFGHIJKLMNOPQRSTUVWXYZ
abcdefghijklmnopqrstuvwxyz
1234567890?!$%&
Studio 231

SALBERTUS TITLING
ABCDEFGHIJKLMNOPQRSTUVWXYZ
1234567890?!$%&
Studio 231

SALBERTUS BOLD TITLING
ABCDEFGHIJKLMNOPQRSTUVWXYZ
1234567890?!$%&
Studio 231

ITC American Typewriter®
ABCDEFGHIJKLMNOPQRSTUVWXYZ
abcdefghijklmnopqrstuvwxyz
1234567890?!$%&
Adobe Systems, Inc.

American Typewriter Bold
ABCDEFGHIJKLMNOPQRSTUVWXYZ
abcdefghijklmnopqrstuvwxyz
1234567890?!$%&

Adobe Systems, Inc.

Americana®
ABCDEFGHIJKLMNOPQRSTUVWXYZ
abcdefghijklmnopqrstuvwxyz
1234567890?!$%&

Adobe Systems, Inc.

Americana Italic
ABCDEFGHIJKLMNOPQRSTUVWXYZ
abcdefghijklmnopqrstuvwxyz
1234567890?!$%&

Adobe Systems, Inc.

Americana Bold
ABCDEFGHIJKLMNOPQRSTUVWXYZ
abcdefghijklmnopqrstuvwxyz
1234567890?!$%&

Adobe Systems, Inc.

Americana Extra Bold
ABCDEFGHIJKLMNOPQRSTUVWXYZ
abcdefghijklmnopqrstuvwxyz
1234567890?!$%&

Adobe Systems, Inc.

SAndromeda
ABCDEFGHIJKLMNOPQRSTUVWXYZ
abcdefghijklmnopqrstuvwxyz
1234567890?!$%&
Studio 231

SAndromeda Extra Bold
ABCDEFGHIJKLMNOPQRSTUVWX
YZabcdefghijklmnopqrstuvwxyz
1234567890?!$%&
Studio 231

SAngular
ABCDEFGHIJKLMNOPQRSTUVWXYZ
abcdefghijklmnopqrstuvwxyz
1234567890?!$%&
Studio 231

SAngular Black
ABCDEFGHIJKLMNOPQRSTUVWXYZ
abcdefghijklmnopqrstuvwxyz
1234567890?!$%&
Studio 231

SAngular Extended
ABCDEFGHIJKLMNOPQRSTUVWXYZ
abcdefghijklmnopqrstuvwxyz
1234567890?!$%&
Studio 231

SAngular Open
ABCDEFGHIJKLMNOPQRSTUVWXYZ
abcdefghijklmnopqrstuvwxyz
1234567890?!$%&
Studio 231

Antique Olive™
ABCDEFGHIJKLMNOPQRSTUVWXYZ
abcdefghijklmnopqrstuvwxyz
1234567890?!$%&
Adobe Systems, Inc.

Antique Olive
ABCDEFGHIJKLMNOPQRSTUVWXYZ
abcdefghijklmnopqrstuvwxyz
1234567890?!$%&
Agfa Corporation

Antique Olive Medium
ABCDEFGHIJKLMNOPQRSTUVWXYZ
abcdefghijklmnopqrstuvwxyz
1234567890?!$%&
Agfa Corporation

Antique Olive Italic
ABCDEFGHIJKLMNOPQRSTUVWXYZ
abcdefghijklmnopqrstuvwxyz
1234567890?!$%&
Adobe Systems, Inc.

Antique Olive Italic
ABCDEFGHIJKLMNOPQRSTUVWXYZ
abcdefghijklmnopqrstuvwxyz
1234567890?!$%&

Agfa Corporation

Antique Olive Medium Italic
ABCDEFGHIJKLMNOPQRSTUVWXYZ
abcdefghijklmnopqrstuvwxyz
1234567890?!$%&

Agfa Corporation

Antique Olive Bold
ABCDEFGHIJKLMNOPQRSTUVWXYZ
abcdefghijklmnopqrstuvwxyz
1234567890?!$%&

Adobe Systems, Inc.

Antique Olive Bold
ABCDEFGHIJKLMNOPQRSTUVWXYZ
abcdefghijklmnopqrstuvwxyz
1234567890?!$%&

Agfa Corporation

Antique Olive Black
ABCDEFGHIJKLMNOPQRSTUVWXYZ
abcdefghijklmnopqrstuvwxyz
1234567890?!$%&

Adobe Systems, Inc.

Antique Olive Light
ABCDEFGHIJKLMNOPQRSTUVWXYZ
abcdefghijklmnopqrstuvwxyz
1234567890?!$%&
Adobe Systems, Inc.

Antique Olive Compact
ABCDEFGHIJKLMNOPQRSTUVWXYZ
abcdefghijklmnopqrstuvwxyz
1234567890?!$%&
Agfa Corporation

Antique Olive Nord
ABCDEFGHIJKLMNOPQRSTUVWXYZ
abcdefghijklmnopqrstuvwxyz
1234567890?!$%&
Agfa Corporation

Antique Olive Nord Italic
ABCDEFGHIJKLMNOPQRSTUVWXYZ
abcdefghijklmnopqrstuvwxyz
1234567890?!$%&
Agfa Corporation

SAnzeigen Grotesk Bold
ABCDEFGHIJKLMNOPQRSTUVWXYZ
abcdefghijklmnopqrstuvwxyz
1234567890?!$%&
Studio 231

31

Aquarius No. 8
ABCDEFGHIJKLMNOPQRSTUVWXYZ
abcdefghijklmnopqrstuvwxyz
1234567890?!$%&
Agfa Corporation

ArchiText
ABCDEFGHIJKLMNOPQRSTUVWXYZ
abcdefghijklmnopqrstuvwxyz
1234567890?!$%&
EmDash

ArchiText Bold
ABCDEFGHIJKLMNOPQRSTUVWXYZ
abcdefghijklmnopqrstuvwxyz
1234567890?!$%&
EmDash

ArchiText Condensed
ABCDEFGHIJKLMNOPQRSTUVWXYZ
abcdefghijklmnopqrstuvwxyz
1234567890?!$%&
EmDash

ArchiText Bold Condensed
ABCDEFGHIJKLMNOPQRSTUVWXYZ
abcdefghijklmnopqrstuvwxyz
1234567890?!$%&
EmDash

Arnold Bocklin

ABCDEFGHIJKLMNOPQRSTUVWXYZ
abcdefghijklmnopqrstuvwxyz
1234567890?!$%&

Adobe Systems, Inc.

Aspen

ABCDEFGHIJKLMNOPQRSTUVWXYZ
abcdefghijklmnopqrstuvwxyz
1234567890?!$%&

Dubl-Click Software, Inc.

Aspen Bold

ABCDEFGHIJKLMNOPQRSTUVWXYZ
abcdefghijklmnopqrstuvwxyz
1234567890?!$%&

Dubl-Click Software, Inc.

Aspen Ultra

ABCDEFGHIJKLMNOPQRSTUVWXYZ
abcdefghijklmnopqrstuvwxyz
1234567890?!$%&

Dubl-Click Software, Inc.

Aukland

ABCDEFGHIJKLMNOPQRSTUVWXYZ
abcdefghijklmnopqrstuvwxyz
1234567890?!$%&

Dubl-Click Software, Inc.

ITC Avant Garde Gothic® Book
ABCDEFGHIJKLMNOPQRSTUVWXYZ
abcdefghijklmnopqrstuvwxyz
1234567890?!$%&

Adobe Systems, Inc.

ITC Avant Garde Gothic Book Oblique
ABCDEFGHIJKLMNOPQRSTUVWXYZ
abcdefghijklmnopqrstuvwxyz
1234567890?!$%&

Adobe Systems, Inc.

ITC Avant Garde Gothic Demi
ABCDEFGHIJKLMNOPQRSTUVWXYZ
abcdefghijklmnopqrstuvwxyz
1234567890?!$%&

Adobe Systems, Inc.

ITC Avant Garde Gothic Demi Oblique
ABCDEFGHIJKLMNOPQRSTUVWXYZ
abcdefghijklmnopqrstuvwxyz
1234567890?!$%&

Adobe Systems, Inc.

Avenir™ 35 Light
ABCDEFGHIJKLMNOPQRSTUVWXYZ
abcdefghijklmnopqrstuvwxyz
1234567890?!$%&

Adobe Systems, Inc.

Avenir 35 Light Oblique
ABCDEFGHIJKLMNOPQRSTUVWXYZ
abcdefghijklmnopqrstuvwxyz
1234567890?!$%&
Adobe Systems, Inc.

Avenir 45 Book
ABCDEFGHIJKLMNOPQRSTUVWXYZ
abcdefghijklmnopqrstuvwxyz
1234567890?!$%&
Adobe Systems, Inc.

Avenir 45 Book Oblique
ABCDEFGHIJKLMNOPQRSTUVWXYZ
abcdefghijklmnopqrstuvwxyz
1234567890?!$%&
Adobe Systems, Inc.

Avenir 55 Roman
ABCDEFGHIJKLMNOPQRSTUVWXYZ
abcdefghijklmnopqrstuvwxyz
1234567890?!$%&
Adobe Systems, Inc.

Avenir 55 Oblique
ABCDEFGHIJKLMNOPQRSTUVWXYZ
abcdefghijklmnopqrstuvwxyz
1234567890?!$%&
Adobe Systems, Inc.

Avenir 65 Medium
ABCDEFGHIJKLMNOPQRSTUVWXYZ
abcdefghijklmnopqrstuvwxyz
1234567890?!$%&
Adobe Systems, Inc.

Avenir 65 Medium Oblique
ABCDEFGHIJKLMNOPQRSTUVWXYZ
abcdefghijklmnopqrstuvwxyz
1234567890?!$%&
Adobe Systems, Inc.

Avenir 85 Heavy
ABCDEFGHIJKLMNOPQRSTUVWXYZ
abcdefghijklmnopqrstuvwxyz
1234567890?!$%&
Adobe Systems, Inc.

Avenir 85 Heavy Oblique
ABCDEFGHIJKLMNOPQRSTUVWXYZ
abcdefghijklmnopqrstuvwxyz
1234567890?!$%&
Adobe Systems, Inc.

Avenir 95 Black
ABCDEFGHIJKLMNOPQRSTUVWXYZ
abcdefghijklmnopqrstuvwxyz
1234567890?!$%&
Adobe Systems, Inc.

Avenir 95 Black Oblique
ABCDEFGHIJKLMNOPQRSTUVWXYZ
abcdefghijklmnopqrstuvwxyz
1234567890?!$%&
Adobe Systems, Inc.

SBaker Argentina No. 1
ABCDEFGHIJKLMNOPQRSTUVWXYZ
abcdefghijklmnopqrstuvwxyz
1234567890?!$%&
Studio 231

SBaker Argentina No. 1 Italic
ABCDEFGHIJKLMNOPQRSTUVWX
YZabcdefghijklmnopqrstuvwxyz
1234567890?!$%&
Studio 231

SBaker Argentina No. 2
ABCDEFGHIJKLMNOPQRSTUVWXYZ
abcdefghijklmnopqrstuvwxyz
1234567890?!$%&
Studio 231

SBaker Argentina No. 2 Italic
ABCDEFGHIJKLMNOPQRSTUVW
XYZabcdefghijklmnopqrstuvwxyz
1234567890?!$%&
Studio 231

SBaker Argentina No. 3
ABCDEFGHIJKLMNOPQRSTUVWXYZ
abcdefghijklmnopqrstuvwxyz
1234567890?!$%&
Studio 231

SBaker Argentina No. 3 Italic
ABCDEFGHIJKLMNOPQRSTUVW
XYZabcdefghijklmnopqrstuvwxyz
1234567890?!$%&
Studio 231

SBaker Argentina No. 4
ABCDEFGHIJKLMNOPQRSTUVWXY
Zabcdefghijklmnopqrstuvwxyz
1234567890?!$%&
Studio 231

SBaker Argentina No. 4 Italic
ABCDEFGHIJKLMNOPQRSTUV
WXYZabcdefghijklmnopqrstuvwxyz
1234567890?!$%&
Studio 231

SBaker Argentina No. 5
ABCDEFGHIJKLMNOPQRSTUVW
XYZabcdefghijklmnopqrstuvwxyz
1234567890?!$%&
Studio 231

38

SBaker Argentina No. 5 Italic
ABCDEFGHIJKLMNOPQRSTU
VWXYZabcdefghijklmnopqrstuvw
xyz1234567890?!$%&
Studio 231

SBaker Argentina No. 6
ABCDEFGHIJKLMNOPQRSTUV
WXYZabcdefghijklmnopqrstuvw
xyz1234567890?!$%&
Studio 231

SBaker Argentina No. 6 Italic
ABCDEFGHIJKLMNOPQRSTU
VWXYZabcdefghijklmnopqrstuv
wxyz1234567890?!$%&
Studio 231

SBaker Danmark One
ABCDEFGHIJKLMNOPQRSTUVWX
YZabcdefghijklmnopqrstuvwxyz
1234567890?!$%&
Studio 231

SBaker Danmark Two
ABCDEFGHIJKLMNOPQRSTUVWX
YZabcdefghijklmnopqrstuvwxyz
1234567890?!$%&
Studio 231

SBaker Danmark Three
ABCDEFGHIJKLMNOPQRSTUVWX
YZabcdefghijklmnopqrstuvwxyz
1234567890?!$%&
Studio 231

SBALLOON EXTRA BOLD
ABCDEFGHIJKLMNOPQRSTUVWXYZ
1234567890?!$%&
Studio 231

SBANCO
ABCDEFGHIJKLMNOPQRSTUVWXYZ
1234567890?!$%&
Studio 231

SBarry Medium
ABCDEFGHIJKLMNOPQRSTUVWXYZ
abcdefghijklmnopqrstuvwxyz
1234567890?!$%&
Studio 231

SBarry Bold
ABCDEFGHIJKLMNOPQRSTUVWXYZ
abcdefghijklmnopqrstuvwxyz
1234567890?!$%&
Studio 231

SBasilea

ABCDEFGHIJKLMNOPQRSTUVWXYZ
abcdefghijklmnopqrstuvwxyz
1234567890?!$%&

Studio 231

Bauer Bodoni Roman

ABCDEFGHIJKLMNOPQRSTUVWXYZ
abcdefghijklmnopqrstuvwxyz
1234567890?!$%&

Adobe Systems, Inc.

Bauer Bodoni Italic

ABCDEFGHIJKLMNOPQRSTUVWXYZ
abcdefghijklmnopqrstuvwxyz
1234567890?!$%&

Adobe Systems, Inc.

Bauer Bodoni® Bold

ABCDEFGHIJKLMNOPQRSTUVWXYZ
abcdefghijklmnopqrstuvwxyz
1234567890?!$%&

Adobe Systems, Inc.

Bauer Bodoni Bold Italic

ABCDEFGHIJKLMNOPQRSTUVWXYZ
abcdefghijklmnopqrstuvwxyz
1234567890?!$%&

Adobe Systems, Inc.

ITC Bauhaus Medium
ABCDEFGHIJKLMNOPQRSTUVWXYZ
abcdefghijklmnopqrstuvwxyz
1234567890?!$%&
Adobe Systems, Inc. / Agfa Corporation

ITC Bauhaus™ Bold
ABCDEFGHIJKLMNOPQRSTUVWXYZ
abcdefghijklmnopqrstuvwxyz
1234567890?!$%&
Adobe Systems, Inc. / Agfa Corporation

ITC Bauhaus Demi
ABCDEFGHIJKLMNOPQRSTUVWXYZ
abcdefghijklmnopqrstuvwxyz
1234567890?!$%&
Adobe Systems, Inc.

ITC Bauhaus Heavy
ABCDEFGHIJKLMNOPQRSTUVWXYZ
abcdefghijklmnopqrstuvwxyz
1234567890?!$%&
Adobe Systems, Inc. / Agfa Corporation

ITC Bauhaus Light
ABCDEFGHIJKLMNOPQRSTUVWXYZ
abcdefghijklmnopqrstuvwxyz
1234567890?!$%&
Adobe Systems, Inc. / Agfa Corporation

SBeads

ABCDEFGHIJKLMNOPQRSTUVWXYZ
abcdefghijklmnopqrstuvwxyz
1234567890?!$%&

Studio 231

Belwe Medium

ABCDEFGHIJKLMNOPQRSTUVWXYZ
abcdefghijklmnopqrstuvwxyz
1234567890?!$%&

Adobe Systems, Inc.

Belwe Bold

ABCDEFGHIJKLMNOPQRSTUVWXYZ
abcdefghijklmnopqrstuvwxyz
1234567890?!$%&

Adobe Systems, Inc.

Belwe Light

ABCDEFGHIJKLMNOPQRSTUVWXYZ
abcdefghijklmnopqrstuvwxyz
1234567890?!$%&

Adobe Systems, Inc.

Belwe Condensed

ABCDEFGHIJKLMNOPQRSTUVWXYZ
abcdefghijklmnopqrstuvwxyz
1234567890?!$%&

Adobe Systems, Inc.

ITC Benguiat®
ABCDEFGHIJKLMNOPQRSTUVWXYZ
abcdefghijklmnopqrstuvwxyz
1234567890?!$%&

Adobe Systems, Inc.

ITC Benguiat Bold
ABCDEFGHIJKLMNOPQRSTUVWXYZ
abcdefghijklmnopqrstuvwxyz
1234567890?!$%&

Adobe Systems, Inc.

ITC Berkeley Oldstyle Book
ABCDEFGHIJKLMNOPQRSTUVWXYZ
abcdefghijklmnopqrstuvwxyz
1234567890?!$%&

Agfa Corporation

ITC Berkeley Oldstyle Book Italic
ABCDEFGHIJKLMNOPQRSTUVWXYZ
abcdefghijklmnopqrstuvwxyz
1234567890?!$%&

Agfa Corporation

ITC Berkeley Oldstyle Bold
ABCDEFGHIJKLMNOPQRSTUVWXYZ
abcdefghijklmnopqrstuvwxyz
1234567890?!$%&

Agfa Corporation

ITC Berkeley Oldstyle Bold Italic
ABCDEFGHIJKLMNOPQRSTUVWXYZ
abcdefghijklmnopqrstuvwxyz
1234567890?!$%&
Agfa Corporation

SBlock
ABCDEFGHIJKLMNOPQRSTUVW
XYZabcdefghijklmnopqrstuvwxy
z1234567890?!$%&
Studio 231

Bodoni
ABCDEFGHIJKLMNOPQRSTUVWXYZ
abcdefghijklmnopqrstuvwxyz
1234567890?!$%&
Adobe Systems, Inc.

Bodoni Italic
ABCDEFGHIJKLMNOPQRSTUVWXYZ
abcdefghijklmnopqrstuvwxyz
1234567890?!$%&
Adobe Systems, Inc.

Bodoni Bold
ABCDEFGHIJKLMNOPQRSTUVWXYZ
abcdefghijklmnopqrstuvwxyz
1234567890?!$%&
Adobe Systems, Inc.

Bodoni Bold Italic
ABCDEFGHIJKLMNOPQRSTUVWXYZ
abcdefghijklmnopqrstuvwxyz
1234567890?!$%&
Adobe Systems, Inc.

Bodoni Poster
ABCDEFGHIJKLMNOPQRSTUVWXYZ
abcdefghijklmnopqrstuvwxyz
1234567890?!$%&
Adobe Systems, Inc.

CG Poster Bodoni
ABCDEFGHIJKLMNOPQRSTUVWXYZ
abcdefghijklmnopqrstuvwxyz
1234567890?!$%&
Agfa Corporation

CG Poster Bodoni Italic
ABCDEFGHIJKLMNOPQRSTUVWXYZ
abcdefghijklmnopqrstuvwxyz
1234567890?!$%&
Agfa Corporation

SBolt Bold
ABCDEFGHIJKLMNOPQRSTUVWXY
ZabcdefghijkImnopqrstuvwxyz
1234567890?!$%&
Studio 231

Bombay

ABCDEFGHIJKLMNOPQRSTUVWXYZ

abcdefghijklmnopqrstuvwxyz

1234567890?!$%&

T/Maker

Bombay Gray

ABCDEFGHIJKLMNOPQRSTUVWXYZ

abcdefghijklmnopqrstuvwxyz

1234567890?!$%&

T/Maker

ITC Bookman® Demi

ABCDEFGHIJKLMNOPQRSTUVWXYZ
abcdefghijklmnopqrstuvwxyz
1234567890?!$%&

Adobe Systems, Inc.

ITC Bookman Demi Italic

ABCDEFGHIJKLMNOPQRSTUVWXYZ
abcdefghijklmnopqrstuvwxyz
1234567890?!$%&

Adobe Systems, Inc.

ITC Bookman Light

ABCDEFGHIJKLMNOPQRSTUVWXYZ
abcdefghijklmnopqrstuvwxyz
1234567890?!$%&

Adobe Systems, Inc.

ITC Bookman Light Italic
ABCDEFGHIJKLMNOPQRSTUVWXYZ
abcdefghijklmnopqrstuvwxyz
1234567890?!$%&.
Adobe Systems, Inc.

SBradley
ABCDEFGHIJKLMNOPQRSTUVWXYZ
abcdefghijklmnopqrstuvwxyz
1234567890?!$%&
Studio 231

SBradley Outline
ABCDEFGHIJKLMNOPQRSTUVWXYZ
abcdefghijklmnopqrstuvwxyz
1234567890?!$%&
Studio 231

SBrody Display
ABCDEFGH99KLMNOPQRSTUVWXY9
abcdefghijklmnopqrstuvwxyz
1234567890?!$%&
Studio 231

Branding Iron
ABCDEFGHIJKLMNOPQRSTUVWXYZ
abcdefghijklmnopqrstuvwxyz
1234567890?!$%&
Agfa Corporation

Briar Book

ABCDEFGHIJKLMNOPQRSTUVWXYZ

abcdefghijklmnopqrstuvwxyz

1234567890?!$%&

EmDash

Briar Bold

ABCDEFGHIJKLMNOPQRSTUVWXYZ

abcdefghijklmnopqrstuvwxyz

1234567890?!$%&

EmDash

Briar Heavy

ABCDEFGHIJKLMNOPQRSTUVWXYZ

abcdefghijklmnopqrstuvwxyz

1234567890?!$%&

EmDash

SBritannic

ABCDEFGHIJKLMNOPQRSTUVWXYZ

abcdefghijklmnopqrstuvwxyz

1234567890?!$%&

Studio 231

SBroadway

ABCDEFGHIJKLMNOPQRSTUVWX
YZabcdefghijklmnopqrstuvwxyz

1234567890?!$%&

Studio 231

SBroadway Engraved
ABCDEFGHIJKLMNOPQRSTUVWX
YZabcdefghijklmnopqrstuvwxyz
1234567890?!$%&

Studio 231

SBRUCE MIKITA
ABCDEFGHIJKLMNOPQRSTUVWXYZ
1234567890?!$%&

Studio 231

Brush Script
ABCDEFGHIJKLMNOP2RSTUVWXYZ
abcdefghijklmnopqrstuvwxyz
1234567890?!$%&

Adobe Systems, Inc.

SBulletin Typewriter
ABCDEFGHIJKLMNOPQRSTUVWXYZ
abcdefghijklmnopqrstuvwxyz
1234567890?!$%&

Studio 231

SBurgondy Right
ABCDEFGHIJKLMNOPQRSTUVWXYZ
abcdefghijklmnopqrstuvwxyz
1234567890?!$%&

Studio 231

SBURXESE BLXCR
XBCDEFGHIXELXNOPQRSTUVWXYZ
1234567890?!$%&
Studio 231

SCactus Bold
ABCDEFGHIJKLMNOPQRSTUVWX
YZabcdefghijklmnopqrstuvwxyz
1234567890?!$%&
Studio 231

SCactus Extra Bold
ABCDEFGHIJKLMNOPQRSTUVW
XYZabcdefghijklmnopqrstuvwx
yz1234567890?!$%&
Studio 231

SCactus Black
ABCDEFGHIJKLMNOPQRSTUVW
XYZabcdefghijklmnopqrstuv
wxyz1234567890?!$%&
Studio 231

SCactus Light
ABCDEFGHIJKLMNOPQRSTUVWXYZ
abcdefghijklmnopqrstuvwxyz
1234567890?!$%&
Studio 231

CALAIS
ABCDEFGHIJKLMNOPQRSTUVWX
YZABCDEFGHIJKLMNOPQRSTU
VWXYZ1234567890?!$%&
Dubl-Click Software, Inc.

CALAIS BOLD
ABCDEFGHIJKLMNOPQRSTUVWX
YZABCDEFGHIJKLMNOPQRSTU
VWXYZ1234567890?!$%&
Dubl-Click Software, Inc.

Candida Roman
ABCDEFGHIJKLMNOPQRSTUVWXYZ
abcdefghijklmnopqrstuvwxyz
1234567890?!$%&
Adobe Systems, Inc.

Candida Italic
ABCDEFGHIJKLMNOPQRSTUVWXYZ
abcdefghijklmnopqrstuvwxyz
1234567890?!$%&
Adobe Systems, Inc.

Candida® Bold
ABCDEFGHIJKLMNOPQRSTUVWXYZ
abcdefghijklmnopqrstuvwxyz
1234567890?!$%&
Adobe Systems, Inc.

SCARTOON BOLD
ABCDEFGHIJKLMNOPQRSTUVWXYZ
1234567890?!$%&
Studio 231

Caslon 3 Roman
ABCDEFGHIJKLMNOPQRSTUVWXYZ
abcdefghijklmnopqrstuvwxyz
1234567890?!$%&
Adobe Systems, Inc.

Caslon 3 Italic
ABCDEFGHIJKLMNOPQRSTUVWXYZ
abcdefghijklmnopqrstuvwxyz
1234567890?!$%&
Adobe Systems, Inc.

Caslon 540 Roman
ABCDEFGHIJKLMNOPQRSTUVWXYZ
abcdefghijklmnopqrstuvwxyz
1234567890?!$%&
Adobe Systems, Inc.

Caslon 540 Italic
ABCDEFGHIJKLMNOPQRSTUVWXYZ
abcdefghijklmnopqrstuvwxyz
1234567890?!$%&
Adobe Systems, Inc.

Caslon Open Face

ABCDEFGHIJKLMNOPQRSTUVWXYZ

abcdefghijklmnopqrstuvwxyz

1234567890?!$%&

Adobe Systems, Inc.

Caspian Book

ABCDEFGHIJKLMNOPQRSTUVWXYZ

abcdefghijklmnopqrstuvwxyz

1234567890?!$%&

EmDash

Caspian Bold

ABCDEFGHIJKLMNOPQRSTUVWXYZ

abcdefghijklmnopqrstuvwxyz

1234567890?!$%&

EmDash

Caspian Condensed

ABCDEFGHIJKLMNOPQRSTUVWXYZ

abcdefghijklmnopqrstuvwxyz

1234567890?!$%&

EmDash

Caspian Bold Condensed

ABCDEFGHIJKLMNOPQRSTUVWXYZ

abcdefghijklmnopqrstuvwxyz

1234567890?!$%&

EmDash

Century Expanded
ABCDEFGHIJKLMNOPQRSTUVWXYZ
abcdefghijklmnopqrstuvwxyz
1234567890?!$%&
Adobe Systems, Inc.

Century Expanded Italic
ABCDEFGHIJKLMNOPQRSTUVWXYZ
abcdefghijklmnopqrstuvwxyz
1234567890?!$%&
Adobe Systems, Inc.

Century Old Style
ABCDEFGHIJKLMNOPQRSTUVWXYZ
abcdefghijklmnopqrstuvwxyz
1234567890?!$%&
Adobe Systems, Inc.

Century Old Style Italic
ABCDEFGHIJKLMNOPQRSTUVWXYZ
abcdefghijklmnopqrstuvwxyz
1234567890?!$%&
Adobe Systems, Inc.

Century Old Style Bold
ABCDEFGHIJKLMNOPQRSTUVWXYZ
abcdefghijklmnopqrstuvwxyz
1234567890?!$%&
Adobe Systems, Inc.

ITC Cheltenham Book
ABCDEFGHIJKLMNOPQRSTUVWXYZ
abcdefghijklmnopqrstuvwxyz
1234567890?!$%&
Adobe Systems, Inc.

ITC Cheltenham Book Italic
ABCDEFGHIJKLMNOPQRSTUVWXYZ
abcdefghijklmnopqrstuvwxyz
1234567890?!$%&
Adobe Systems, Inc.

ITC Cheltenham® Bold
ABCDEFGHIJKLMNOPQRSTUVWXYZ
abcdefghijklmnopqrstuvwxyz
1234567890?!$%&
Adobe Systems, Inc.

ITC Cheltenham Bold Italic
ABCDEFGHIJKLMNOPQRSTUVWXYZ
abcdefghijklmnopqrstuvwxyz
1234567890?!$%&
Adobe Systems, Inc.

SCHINA
ABCDEFGHIJKLMNOPQR
STUVWXYZ
1234567890?!$%&
Studio 231

Clarendon™
ABCDEFGHIJKLMNOPQRSTUVWXYZ
abcdefghijklmnopqrstuvwxyz
1234567890?!$%&
Adobe Systems, Inc.

Clarendon Bold
ABCDEFGHIJKLMNOPQRSTUVWXYZ
abcdefghijklmnopqrstuvwxyz
1234567890?!$%&
Adobe Systems, Inc.

Clarendon Light
ABCDEFGHIJKLMNOPQRSTUVWXYZ
abcdefghijklmnopqrstuvwxyz
1234567890?!$%&
Adobe Systems, Inc.

Clarendon Book Condensed
ABCDEFGHIJKLMNOPQRSTUVWXYZ
abcdefghijklmnopqrstuvwxyz
1234567890?!$%&
Agfa Corporation

ITC Clearface Regular
ABCDEFGHIJKLMNOPQRSTUVWXYZ
abcdefghijklmnopqrstuvwxyz
1234567890?!$%&
Adobe Systems, Inc. / Agfa Corporation

ITC Clearface Regular Italic
ABCDEFGHIJKLMNOPQRSTUVWXYZ
abcdefghijklmnopqrstuvwxyz
1234567890?!$%&
Adobe Systems, Inc. / Agfa Corporation

ITC Clearface Bold
ABCDEFGHIJKLMNOPQRSTUVWXYZ
abcdefghijklmnopqrstuvwxyz
1234567890?!$%&
Adobe Systems, Inc. / Agfa Corporation

ITC Clearface® Black
ABCDEFGHIJKLMNOPQRSTUVWXYZ
abcdefghijklmnopqrstuvwxyz
1234567890?!$%&
Adobe Systems, Inc.

ITC Clearface Heavy
ABCDEFGHIJKLMNOPQRSTUVWXYZ
abcdefghijklmnopqrstuvwxyz
1234567890?!$%&
Adobe Systems, Inc.

ITC Clearface Bold Italic
ABCDEFGHIJKLMNOPQRSTUVWXYZ
abcdefghijklmnopqrstuvwxyz
1234567890?!$%&
Adobe Systems, Inc. / Agfa Corporation

ITC Clearface Black Italic
ABCDEFGHIJKLMNOPQRSTUVWXYZ
abcdefghijklmnopqrstuvwxyz
1234567890?!$%&

Adobe Systems, Inc.

ITC Clearface Heavy Italic
ABCDEFGHIJKLMNOPQRSTUVWXYZ
abcdefghijklmnopqrstuvwxyz
1234567890?!$%&

Adobe Systems, Inc.

SCloister Open Face
ABCDEFGHIJKLMNOPQRSTUVWX
YZabcdefghijklmnopqrstuvwxyz
1234567890?!$%&

Studio 231

Cochin™
ABCDEFGHIJKLMNOPQRSTUVWXYZ
abcdefghijklmnopqrstuvwxyz
1234567890?!$%&

Adobe Systems, Inc.

Cochin Italic
ABCDEFGHIJKLMNOPQRSTUVWXYZ
abcdefghijklmnopqrstuvwxyz
1234567890?!$%&

Adobe Systems, Inc.

Cochin Bold

ABCDEFGHIJKLMNOPQRSTUVWXYZ
abcdefghijklmnopqrstuvwxyz
1234567890?!$%&

Adobe Systems, Inc.

Cochin Bold Italic

ABCDEFGHIJKLMNOPQRSTUVWXYZ

abcdefghijklmnopqrstuvwxyz

1234567890?!$%e3

Adobe Systems, Inc.

CG Collage

ABCDEFGHIJKLMNOPQRSTUVWXYZ
abcdefghijklmnopqrstuvwxyz
1234567890?!$ % &

Agfa Corporation

CG Collage Italic

ABCDEFGHIJKLMNOPQRSTUVWXYZ

abcdefghijklmnopqrstuvwxyz

1234567890?!$%e3

Agfa Corporation

CG Collage Bold

ABCDEFGHIJKLMNOPQRSTUVWXYZ
abcdefghijklmnopqrstuvwxyz
1234567890?!$ % &

Agfa Corporation

CG Collage Bold Italic
ABCDEFGHIJKLMNOPQRSTUVWXYZ
abcdefghijklmnopqrstuvwxyz
1234567890?!$%&

Agfa Corporation

Concorde®
ABCDEFGHIJKLMNOPQRSTUVWXYZ
abcdefghijklmnopqrstuvwxyz
1234567890?!$%&

Adobe Systems, Inc.

Concorde Italic
ABCDEFGHIJKLMNOPQRSTUVWXYZ
abcdefghijklmnopqrstuvwxyz
1234567890?!$%&

Adobe Systems, Inc.

Concorde Bold
ABCDEFGHIJKLMNOPQRSTUVWXYZ
abcdefghijklmnopqrstuvwxyz
1234567890?!$%&

Adobe Systems, Inc.

Concorde Bold Italic
ABCDEFGHIJKLMNOPQRSTUVWXYZ
abcdefghijklmnopqrstuvwxyz
1234567890?!$%&

Adobe Systems, Inc.

Cooper Black
ABCDEFGHIJKLMNOPQRSTUVWXYZ
abcdefghijklmnopqrstuvwxyz
1234567890?!$%&
Adobe Systems, Inc.

Cooper Black Italic
ABCDEFGHIJKLMNOPQRSTUVWXYZ
abcdefghijklmnopqrstuvwxyz
1234567890?!$%&
Adobe Systems, Inc.

Corona™
ABCDEFGHIJKLMNOPQRSTUVWXYZ
abcdefghijklmnopqrstuvwxyz
1234567890?!$%&
Adobe Systems, Inc.

Corona Italic
ABCDEFGHIJKLMNOPQRSTUVWXYZ
abcdefghijklmnopqrstuvwxyz
1234567890?!$%&
Adobe Systems, Inc.

Corona Bold
ABCDEFGHIJKLMNOPQRSTUVWXYZ
abcdefghijklmnopqrstuvwxyz
1234567890?!$%&
Adobe Systems, Inc.

SCORNBALL
ABCDEFGHIJKLMNOPQRSTUVWXY
Z1234567890?!$%&
Studio 231

Dom Casual
ABCDEFGHIJKLMNOPQRSTUVWXYZ
abcdefghijklmnopqrstuvwxyz
1234567890?!$%&
Adobe Systems, Inc.

Dom Casual Bold
ABCDEFGHIJKLMNOPQRSTUVWXYZ
abcdefghijklmnopqrstuvwxyz
1234567890?!$%&
Adobe Systems, Inc.

SDUO SOLID
ABCDEFGHIJKLMNOPQRSTUVWX
YZ1234567890?!$%&
Studio 231

Egyptian Bold Condensed
ABCDEFGHIJKLMNOPQRSTUVWXYZ
abcdefghijklmnopqrstuvwxyz
1234567890?!$%&
Alphabets, Inc.

Small Egyptian Bold Condensed
ABCDEFGHIJKLMNOPQRSTUVWXYZ
abcdefghijklmnopqrstuvwxyz
1234567890?!$%&
Alphabets, Inc.

VCG Egyptian 505
ABCDEFGHIJKLMNOPQRSTUVWXYZ
abcdefghijklmnopqrstuvwxyz
1234567890?!$%&
Agfa Corporation

VCG Egyptian 505 Medium
ABCDEFGHIJKLMNOPQRSTUVWXYZ
abcdefghijklmnopqrstuvwxyz
1234567890?!$%&
Agfa Corporation

VCG Egyptian 505 Bold
ABCDEFGHIJKLMNOPQRSTUVWXYZ
abcdefghijklmnopqrstuvwxyz
1234567890?!$%&
Agfa Corporation

VCG Egyptian 505 Light
ABCDEFGHIJKLMNOPQRSTUVWXYZ
abcdefghijklmnopqrstuvwxyz
1234567890?!$%&
Agfa Corporation

ITC Eras Book
ABCDEFGHIJKLMNOPQRSTUVWXYZ
abcdefghijklmnopqrstuvwxyz
1234567890?!$%&
Adobe Systems, Inc.

ITC Eras Medium
ABCDEFGHIJKLMNOPQRSTUVWXYZ
abcdefghijklmnopqrstuvwxyz
1234567890?!$%&
Adobe Systems, Inc.

ITC Eras® Bold
ABCDEFGHIJKLMNOPQRSTUVWXYZ
abcdefghijklmnopqrstuvwxyz
1234567890?!$%&
Adobe Systems, Inc.

ITC Eras Demi
ABCDEFGHIJKLMNOPQRSTUVWXYZ
abcdefghijklmnopqrstuvwxyz
1234567890?!$%&
Adobe Systems, Inc.

ITC Eras Ultra
ABCDEFGHIJKLMNOPQRSTUVWXYZ
abcdefghijklmnopqrstuvwxyz
1234567890?!$%&
Adobe Systems, Inc.

ITC Eras Light
ABCDEFGHIJKLMNOPQRSTUVWXYZ
abcdefghijklmnopqrstuvwxyz
1234567890?!$%&
Adobe Systems, Inc.

Eurostile®
ABCDEFGHIJKLMNOPQRSTUVWXYZ
abcdefghijklmnopqrstuvwxyz
1234567890?!$%&
Adobe Systems, Inc.

Eurostile Oblique
ABCDEFGHIJKLMNOPQRSTUVWXYZ
abcdefghijklmnopqrstuvwxyz
1234567890?!$%&
Adobe Systems, Inc.

Eurostile Bold
ABCDEFGHIJKLMNOPQRSTUVWXYZ
abcdefghijklmnopqrstuvwxyz
1234567890?!$%&
Adobe Systems, Inc.

Eurostile Demi
ABCDEFGHIJKLMNOPQRSTUVWXYZ
abcdefghijklmnopqrstuvwxyz
1234567890?!$%&
Adobe Systems, Inc.

Eurostile Bold Oblique
ABCDEFGHIJKLMNOPQRSTUVWXYZ
abcdefghijklmnopqrstuvwxyz
1234567890?!$%&
Adobe Systems, Inc.

Eurostile Demi Oblique
ABCDEFGHIJKLMNOPQRSTUVWXYZ
abcdefghijklmnopqrstuvwxyz
1234567890?!$%&
Adobe Systems, Inc.

Excelsior™
ABCDEFGHIJKLMNOPQRSTUVWXYZ
abcdefghijklmnopqrstuvwxyz
1234567890?!$%&
Adobe Systems, Inc.

Excelsior Italic
ABCDEFGHIJKLMNOPQRSTUVWXYZ
abcdefghijklmnopqrstuvwxyz
1234567890?!$%&
Adobe Systems, Inc.

Excelsior Bold
ABCDEFGHIJKLMNOPQRSTUVWXYZ
abcdefghijklmnopqrstuvwxyz
1234567890?!$%&
Adobe Systems, Inc.

ITC Fenice Regular
ABCDEFGHIJKLMNOPQRSTUVWXYZ
abcdefghijklmnopqrstuvwxyz
1234567890?!$%&
Agfa Corporation

ITC Fenice Regular Italic
ABCDEFGHIJKLMNOPQRSTUVWXYZ
abcdefghijklmnopqrstuvwxyz
1234567890?!$%&
Agfa Corporation

ITC Fenice Bold
ABCDEFGHIJKLMNOPQRSTUVWXYZ
abcdefghijklmnopqrstuvwxyz
1234567890?!$%&
Agfa Corporation

ITC Fenice Bold Italic
ABCDEFGHIJKLMNOPQRSTUVWXYZ
abcdefghijklmnopqrstuvwxyz
1234567890?!$%&
Agfa Corporation

Fette Fraktur
ABCDEFGHIJKLMNOPQRSTUVWXYZ
abcdefghijklmnopqrstuvwxyz
1234567890?!$%&
Adobe Systems, Inc.

Folio Medium

ABCDEFGHIJKLMNOPQRSTUVWXYZ

abcdefghijklmnopqrstuvwxyz

1234567890?!$%&

Adobe Systems, Inc.

Folio® Bold

ABCDEFGHIJKLMNOPQRSTUVWXYZ

abcdefghijklmnopqrstuvwxyz

1234567890?!$%&

Adobe Systems, Inc.

Folio Extra Bold

ABCDEFGHIJKLMNOPQRSTUVWXYZ

abcdefghijklmnopqrstuvwxyz

1234567890?!$%&

Adobe Systems, Inc.

Folio Light

ABCDEFGHIJKLMNOPQRSTUVWXYZ

abcdefghijklmnopqrstuvwxyz

1234567890?!$%&

Adobe Systems, Inc.

Folio Bold Condensed

ABCDEFGHIJKLMNOPQRSTUVWXYZ

abcdefghijklmnopqrstuvwxyz

1234567890?!$%&

Adobe Systems, Inc.

SFolkwang
ABCDEFGHIJKLMNOPQRSTUVWXYZ
abcdefghijklmnopqrstuvwxyz
1234567890?!$%&
Studio 231

Frankfurt
ABCDEFGHIJKLMNOPQRSTUVWXYZ
abcdefghijklmnopqrstuvwxyz
1234567890?!$%&
Dubl-Click Software, Inc.

Frankfurt Medium
ABCDEFGHIJKLMNOPQRSTUVWXYZ
abcdefghijklmnopqrstuvwxyz
1234567890?!$%&
Dubl-Click Software, Inc.

Frankfurt Bold
ABCDEFGHIJKLMNOPQRSTUVWXYZ
abcdefghijklmnopqrstuvwxyz
1234567890?!$%&
Dubl-Click Software, Inc.

Frankfurt Ultra
ABCDEFGHIJKLMNOPQRSTUVWXYZ
abcdefghijklmnopqrstuvwxyz
1234567890?!$%&
Dubl-Click Software, Inc.

Franklin Gothic No. 2 Roman
ABCDEFGHIJKLMNOPQRSTUVWXYZ
abcdefghijklmnopqrstuvwxyz
1234567890?!$%&
Adobe Systems, Inc.

Franklin Gothic Condensed
ABCDEFGHIJKLMNOPQRSTUVWXYZ
abcdefghijklmnopqrstuvwxyz
1234567890?!$%&
Adobe Systems, Inc.

Franklin Gothic Extra Condensed
ABCDEFGHIJKLMNOPQRSTUVWXYZ
abcdefghijklmnopqrstuvwxyz
1234567890?!$%&
Adobe Systems, Inc.

ITC Franklin Gothic® Book
ABCDEFGHIJKLMNOPQRSTUVWXYZ
abcdefghijklmnopqrstuvwxyz
1234567890?!$%&
Adobe Systems, Inc.

ITC Franklin Gothic Book Oblique
ABCDEFGHIJKLMNOPQRSTUVWXYZ
abcdefghijklmnopqrstuvwxyz
1234567890?!$%&
Adobe Systems, Inc.

71

ITC Franklin Gothic Demi
ABCDEFGHIJKLMNOPQRSTUVWXYZ
abcdefghijklmnopqrstuvwxyz
1234567890?!$%&
Adobe Systems, Inc.

ITC Franklin Gothic Heavy
ABCDEFGHIJKLMNOPQRSTUVWXYZ
abcdefghijklmnopqrstuvwxyz
1234567890?!$%&
Adobe Systems, Inc.

ITC Franklin Gothic Demi Oblique
ABCDEFGHIJKLMNOPQRSTUVWXYZ
abcdefghijklmnopqrstuvwxyz
1234567890?!$%&
Adobe Systems, Inc.

ITC Franklin Gothic Heavy Oblique
ABCDEFGHIJKLMNOPQRSTUVWXYZ
abcdefghijklmnopqrstuvwxyz
1234567890?!$%&
Adobe Systems, Inc.

SFreehand
ABCDEFGHIJKLMNOPQRSTUVWXYZ
abcdefghijklmnopqrstuvwxyz
1234567890?!$%&
Studio 231

Freestyle Script
ABCDEFGHIJKLMNOPQRSTUVWXYZ
abcdefghijklmnopqrstuvwxyz
1234567890?!$%&
Adobe Systems, Inc.

ITC Friz Quadrata®
ABCDEFGHIJKLMNOPQRSTUVWXYZ
abcdefghijklmnopqrstuvwxyz
1234567890?!$%&
Adobe Systems, Inc.

ITC Friz Quadrata Bold
ABCDEFGHIJKLMNOPQRSTUVWXYZ
abcdefghijklmnopqrstuvwxyz
1234567890?!$%&
Adobe Systems, Inc.

CG Frontiera 55
ABCDEFGHIJKLMNOPQRSTUVWXYZ
abcdefghijklmnopqrstuvwxyz
1234567890?!$%&
Agfa Corporation

CG Frontiera 56
ABCDEFGHIJKLMNOPQRSTUVWXYZ
abcdefghijklmnopqrstuvwxyz
1234567890?!$%&
Agfa Corporation

CG Frontiera 65
ABCDEFGHIJKLMNOPQRSTUVWXYZ
abcdefghijklmnopqrstuvwxyz
1234567890?!$%&
Agfa Corporation

CG Frontiera 66
ABCDEFGHIJKLMNOPQRSTUVWXYZ
abcdefghijklmnopqrstuvwxyz
1234567890?!$%&
Agfa Corporation

SFrozen Alaska
ABCDEFGHIJKLMNOPQRSTUVWXYZ
abcdefghijklmnopqrstuvwxyz
1234567890?!$%&
Studio 231

Frutiger™ 45 Light
ABCDEFGHIJKLMNOPQRSTUVWXYZ
abcdefghijklmnopqrstuvwxyz
1234567890?!$%&
Adobe Systems, Inc.

Frutiger 46 Light Italic
ABCDEFGHIJKLMNOPQRSTUVWXYZ
abcdefghijklmnopqrstuvwxyz
1234567890?!$%&
Adobe Systems, Inc.

Frutiger 55

ABCDEFGHIJKLMNOPQRSTUVWXYZ
abcdefghijklmnopqrstuvwxyz
1234567890?!$%&
Adobe Systems, Inc.

Frutiger 56 Italic

ABCDEFGHIJKLMNOPQRSTUVWXYZ
abcdefghijklmnopqrstuvwxyz
1234567890?!$%&
Adobe Systems, Inc.

Frutiger 65 Bold

ABCDEFGHIJKLMNOPQRSTUVWXYZ
abcdefghijklmnopqrstuvwxyz
1234567890?!$%&
Adobe Systems, Inc.

Frutiger 66 Bold Italic

ABCDEFGHIJKLMNOPQRSTUVWXYZ
abcdefghijklmnopqrstuvwxyz
1234567890?!$%&
Adobe Systems, Inc.

Frutiger 75 Black

ABCDEFGHIJKLMNOPQRSTUVWXYZ
abcdefghijklmnopqrstuvwxyz
1234567890?!$%&
Adobe Systems, Inc.

Frutiger 76 Black Italic
ABCDEFGHIJKLMNOPQRSTUVWXYZ
abcdefghijklmnopqrstuvwxyz
1234567890?!$%&
Adobe Systems, Inc.

Frutiger 95 Ultra Black
ABCDEFGHIJKLMNOPQRSTUVWXYZ
abcdefghijklmnopqrstuvwxyz
1234567890?!$%&
Adobe Systems, Inc.

Futura
ABCDEFGHIJKLMNOPQRSTUVWXYZ
abcdefghijklmnopqrstuvwxyz
1234567890?!$%&
Adobe Systems, Inc.

Futura Book
ABCDEFGHIJKLMNOPQRSTUVWXYZ
abcdefghijklmnopqrstuvwxyz
1234567890?!$%&
Adobe Systems, Inc.

Futura Oblique
ABCDEFGHIJKLMNOPQRSTUVWXYZ
abcdefghijklmnopqrstuvwxyz
1234567890?!$%&
Adobe Systems, Inc.

Futura Book Oblique
ABCDEFGHIJKLMNOPQRSTUVWXYZ
abcdefghijklmnopqrstuvwxyz
1234567890?!$%&
Adobe Systems, Inc.

Futura® Bold
ABCDEFGHIJKLMNOPQRSTUVWXYZ
abcdefghijklmnopqrstuvwxyz
1234567890?!$%&
Adobe Systems, Inc.

Futura Extra Bold
ABCDEFGHIJKLMNOPQRSTUVWXYZ
abcdefghijklmnopqrstuvwxyz
1234567890?!$%&
Adobe Systems, Inc.

SFutura Black
ABCDEFGHIJKLMNOPQRSTUVWXYZ
abcdefghijklmnopqrstuvwxyz
1234567890?!$%&
Studio 231

Futura Heavy
ABCDEFGHIJKLMNOPQRSTUVWXYZ
abcdefghijklmnopqrstuvwxyz
1234567890?!$%&
Adobe Systems, Inc.

77

Futura Bold Oblique
ABCDEFGHIJKLMNOPQRSTUVWXYZ
abcdefghijklmnopqrstuvwxyz
1234567890?!$%&
Adobe Systems, Inc.

Futura Extra Bold Oblique
ABCDEFGHIJKLMNOPQRSTUVWXYZ
abcdefghijklmnopqrstuvwxyz
1234567890?!$%&
Adobe Systems, Inc.

Futura Heavy Oblique
ABCDEFGHIJKLMNOPQRSTUVWXYZ
abcdefghijklmnopqrstuvwxyz
1234567890?!$%&
Adobe Systems, Inc.

Futura Light
ABCDEFGHIJKLMNOPQRSTUVWXYZ
abcdefghijklmnopqrstuvwxyz
1234567890?!$%&
Adobe Systems, Inc.

Futura Light Oblique
ABCDEFGHIJKLMNOPQRSTUVWXYZ
abcdefghijklmnopqrstuvwxyz
1234567890?!$%&
Adobe Systems, Inc.

Futura Condensed

ABCDEFGHIJKLMNOPQRSTUVWXYZ

abcdefghijklmnopqrstuvwxyz

1234567890?!$%&

Adobe Systems, Inc.

Futura Condensed Oblique

ABCDEFGHIJKLMNOPQRSTUVWXYZ

abcdefghijklmnopqrstuvwxyz

1234567890?!$%&

Adobe Systems, Inc.

Futura Condensed Bold

ABCDEFGHIJKLMNOPQRSTUVWXYZ

abcdefghijklmnopqrstuvwxyz

1234567890?!$%&

Adobe Systems, Inc.

Futura Condensed Extra Bold

ABCDEFGHIJKLMNOPQRSTUVWXYZ

abcdefghijklmnopqrstuvwxyz

1234567890?!$%&

Adobe Systems, Inc.

Futura Condensed Bold Oblique

ABCDEFGHIJKLMNOPQRSTUVWXYZ

abcdefghijklmnopqrstuvwxyz

1234567890?!$%&

Adobe Systems, Inc.

Futura Condensed Extra Bold Oblique
ABCDEFGHIJKLMNOPQRSTUVWXYZ
abcdefghijklmnopqrstuvwxyz
1234567890?!$%&
Adobe Systems, Inc.

Futura Condensed Light
ABCDEFGHIJKLMNOPQRSTUVWXYZ
abcdefghijklmnopqrstuvwxyz
1234567890?!$%&
Adobe Systems, Inc.

Futura Condensed Light Oblique
ABCDEFGHIJKLMNOPQRSTUVWXYZ
abcdefghijklmnopqrstuvwxyz
1234567890?!$%&
Adobe Systems, Inc.

SGALLIA
ABCDEFGHIJKLMNOPQRSTUV
WXYZ1234567890?!$%&
Studio 231

ITC Galliard Roman
ABCDEFGHIJKLMNOPQRSTUVWXYZ
abcdefghijklmnopqrstuvwxyz
1234567890?!$%&
Adobe Systems, Inc.

ITC Galliard Italic
ABCDEFGHIJKLMNOPQRSTUVWXYZ
abcdefghijklmnopqrstuvwxyz
1234567890?!$%&
Adobe Systems, Inc.

ITC Galliard® Bold
ABCDEFGHIJKLMNOPQRSTUVWXYZ
abcdefghijklmnopqrstuvwxyz
1234567890?!$%&
Adobe Systems, Inc.

ITC Galliard Bold Italic
ABCDEFGHIJKLMNOPQRSTUVWXYZ
abcdefghijklmnopqrstuvwxyz
1234567890?!$%&
Adobe Systems, Inc.

Adobe Garamond Regular
ABCDEFGHIJKLMNOPQRSTUVWXYZ
abcdefghijklmnopqrstuvwxyz
1234567890?!$%&
Adobe Systems, Inc.

Adobe Garamond Italic
ABCDEFGHIJKLMNOPQRSTUVWXYZ
abcdefghijklmnopqrstuvwxyz
1234567890?!$%&
Adobe Systems, Inc.

Adobe Garamond™ Bold
ABCDEFGHIJKLMNOPQRSTUVWXYZ
abcdefghijklmnopqrstuvwxyz
1234567890?!$%&
Adobe Systems, Inc.

Adobe Garamond Semibold
ABCDEFGHIJKLMNOPQRSTUVWXYZ
abcdefghijklmnopqrstuvwxyz
1234567890?!$%&
Adobe Systems, Inc.

Adobe Garamond Bold Italic
ABCDEFGHIJKLMNOPQRSTUVWXYZ
abcdefghijklmnopqrstuvwxyz
1234567890?!$%&
Adobe Systems, Inc.

Adobe Garamond Semibold Italic
ABCDEFGHIJKLMNOPQRSTUVWXYZ
abcdefghijklmnopqrstuvwxyz
1234567890?!$%&
Adobe Systems, Inc.

ADOBE GARAMOND EXPERT COLLECTION
ABCDEFGHIJKLMNOPQRSTUVWXYZ
ABCDEFGHIJKLMNOPQRSTUVWXYZ
Adobe Systems, Inc.

Garamond 3™

ABCDEFGHIJKLMNOPQRSTUVWXYZ
abcdefghijklmnopqrstuvwxyz
1234567890?!$%&
Adobe Systems, Inc.

Garamond 3 Italic

ABCDEFGHIJKLMNOPQRSTUVWXYZ
abcdefghijklmnopqrstuvwxyz
1234567890?!$%&
Adobe Systems, Inc.

Garamond 3 Bold

ABCDEFGHIJKLMNOPQRSTUVWXYZ
abcdefghijklmnopqrstuvwxyz
1234567890?!$%&
Adobe Systems, Inc.

Garamond 3 Bold Italic

ABCDEFGHIJKLMNOPQRSTUVWXYZ
abcdefghijklmnopqrstuvwxyz
1234567890?!$%&
Adobe Systems, Inc.

Garamond Antiqua

ABCDEFGHIJKLMNOPQRSTUVWXYZ
abcdefghijklmnopqrstuvwxyz
1234567890?!$%&
Agfa Corporation

ITC Garamond® Bold
ABCDEFGHIJKLMNOPQRSTUVWXYZ
abcdefghijklmnopqrstuvwxyz
1234567890?!$%&
Adobe Systems, Inc.

ITC Garamond Bold Italic
ABCDEFGHIJKLMNOPQRSTUVWXYZ
abcdefghijklmnopqrstuvwxyz
1234567890?!$%&
Adobe Systems, Inc.

ITC Garamond Light
ABCDEFGHIJKLMNOPQRSTUVWXYZ
abcdefghijklmnopqrstuvwxyz
1234567890?!$%&
Adobe Systems, Inc.

ITC Garamond Light Italic
ABCDEFGHIJKLMNOPQRSTUVWXYZ
abcdefghijklmnopqrstuvwxyz
1234567890?!$%&
Adobe Systems, Inc.

Garamond Halbfett
ABCDEFGHIJKLMNOPQRSTUVWXYZ
abcdefghijklmnopqrstuvwxyz
1234567890?!$%&
Agfa Corporation

Garamond Kursiv
ABCDEFGHIJKLMNOPQRSTUVWXYZ
abcdefghijklmnopqrstuvwxyz
1234567890?!$%&
Agfa Corporation

Garamond Kursiv Halbfett
ABCDEFGHIJKLMNOPQRSTUVWXYZ
abcdefghijklmnopqrstuvwxyz
1234567890?!$%&
Agfa Corporation

Stempel Garamond™ Roman
ABCDEFGHIJKLMNOPQRSTUVWXYZ
abcdefghijklmnopqrstuvwxyz
1234567890?!$%&
Adobe Systems, Inc.

Stempel Garamond Italic
ABCDEFGHIJKLMNOPQRSTUVWXYZ
abcdefghijklmnopqrstuvwxyz
1234567890?!$%&
Adobe Systems, Inc.

Stempel Garamond Bold
ABCDEFGHIJKLMNOPQRSTUVWXYZ
abcdefghijklmnopqrstuvwxyz
1234567890?!$%&
Adobe Systems, Inc.

Stempel Garamond Bold Italic
ABCDEFGHIJKLMNOPQRSTUVWXYZ
abcdefghijklmnopqrstuvwxyz
1234567890?!$%&
Adobe Systems, Inc.

Garth Graphic
ABCDEFGHIJKLMNOPQRSTUVWXYZ
abcdefghijklmnopqrstuvwxyz
1234567890?!$%&
Agfa Corporation

Garth Graphic Italic
ABCDEFGHIJKLMNOPQRSTUVWXYZ
abcdefghijklmnopqrstuvwxyz
1234567890?!$%&
Agfa Corporation

Garth Graphic Bold
ABCDEFGHIJKLMNOPQRSTUVWXYZ
abcdefghijklmnopqrstuvwxyz
1234567890?!$%&
Agfa Corporation

Garth Graphic Bold Italic
ABCDEFGHIJKLMNOPQRSTUVWXYZ
abcdefghijklmnopqrstuvwxyz
1234567890?!$%&
Agfa Corporation

GENDARME HEAVY™
ABCDEFGHIJKLMNOPQRSTUVWXY
ZABCDEFGHIJKLMNOPQRSTUVWXYZ
1234567890?!$%&
EmDash

SGill Sans
ABCDEFGHIJKLMNOPQRSTUVWXYZ
abcdefghijklmnopqrstuvwxyz
1234567890?!$%&
Studio 231

SGill Sans Italic
ABCDEFGHIJKLMNOPQRSTUVWXYZ
abcdefghijklmnopqrstuvwxyz
1234567890?!$%&
Studio 231

SGill Sans Bold
ABCDEFGHIJKLMNOPQRSTUVWXY
Zabcdefghijklmnopqrstuvwxyz
1234567890?!$%&
Studio 231

SGill Sans Extra Bold
ABCDEFGHIJKLMNOPQRSTUVWX
YZabcdefghijklmnopqrstuvwxyz
1234567890?!$%&
Studio 231

SGill Sans Ultra Bold
ABCDEFGHIJKLMNOPQRSTUVW
XYZabcdefghijklmnopqrstuv
wxyz1234567890?!$%&
Studio 231

SGill Sans Bold Italic
ABCDEFGHI JKLMNOPQRSTUVW XYZ
abcdefghi jklmnopqrstuvw xyz
1234567890?!$%&
Studio 231

SGill Sans Light
ABCDEFGHIJKLMNOPQRSTUVWXYZ
abcdefghijklmnopqrstuvwxyz
1234567890?!$%&
Studio 231

SGill Sans Light Italic
ABCDEFGHI JKLMNOPQRSTUVWXYZ
abcdefghi jklmnopqrstuvwxyz
1234567890?!$%&
Studio 231

SGill Sans Bold Condensed
ABCDEFGHIJKLMNOPQRSTUVWXYZ
abcdefghijklmnopqrstuvwxyz
1234567890?!$%&
Studio 231

SGill Sans Extra Bold Condensed
ABCDEFGHIJKLMNOPQRSTUVWXYZ
abcdefghijklmnopqrstuvwxyz
1234567890?!$%&

Studio 231

Globe Gothic Bold
ABCDEFGHIJKLMNOPQRSTUVWXYZ
abcdefghijklmnopqrstuvwxyz
1234567890?!$%&

Agfa Corporation

Globe Gothic Demi
ABCDEFGHIJKLMNOPQRSTUVWXYZ
abcdefghijklmnopqrstuvwxyz
1234567890?!$%&

Agfa Corporation

Globe Gothic Ultra
ABCDEFGHIJKLMNOPQRSTUVWXYZ
abcdefghijklmnopqrstuvwxyz
1234567890?!$%&

Agfa Corporation

Globe Gothic Light
ABCDEFGHIJKLMNOPQRSTUVWXYZ
abcdefghijklmnopqrstuvwxyz
1234567890?!$%&

Agfa Corporation

Glypha™

ABCDEFGHIJKLMNOPQRSTUVWXYZ
abcdefghijklmnopqrstuvwxyz
1234567890?!$%&

Adobe Systems, Inc.

Glypha Oblique

ABCDEFGHIJKLMNOPQRSTUVWXYZ
abcdefghijklmnopqrstuvwxyz
1234567890?!$%&

Adobe Systems, Inc.

Glypha Bold

ABCDEFGHIJKLMNOPQRSTUVWXYZ
abcdefghijklmnopqrstuvwxyz
1234567890?!$%&

Adobe Systems, Inc.

Glypha Bold Oblique

ABCDEFGHIJKLMNOPQRSTUVWXYZ
abcdefghijklmnopqrstuvwxyz
1234567890?!$%&

Adobe Systems, Inc.

Gothic 13

ABCDEFGHIJKLMNOPQRSTUVWXYZ
abcdefghijklmnopqrstuvwxyz
1234567890?!$%&

Adobe Systems, Inc.

Goudy Extra Bold

ABCDEFGHIJKLMNOPQRSTUVWXYZ
abcdefghijklmnopqrstuvwxyz
1234567890?!$%&

Adobe Systems, Inc.

Goudy Heavyface

ABCDEFGHIJKLMNOPQRSTUVWXYZ
abcdefghijklmnopqrstuvwxyz
1234567890?!$%&

Adobe Systems, Inc.

Goudy Heavyface

ABCDEFGHIJKLMNOPQRSTUVWXYZ
abcdefghijklmnopqrstuvwxyz
1234567890?!$%&

Agfa Corporation

Goudy Heavyface Italic

ABCDEFGHIJKLMNOPQRSTUVWXYZ
abcdefghijklmnopqrstuvwxyz
1234567890?!$%&

Adobe Systems, Inc.

Goudy Heavyface Italic

ABCDEFGHIJKLMNOPQRSTUVWXYZ
abcdefghijklmnopqrstuvwxyz
1234567890?!$%&

Agfa Corporation

Goudy Heavyface Condensed
ABCDEFGHIJKLMNOPQRSTUVWXYZ
abcdefghijklmnopqrstuvwxyz
1234567890?!$%&
Agfa Corporation

Goudy Old Style
ABCDEFGHIJKLMNOPQRSTUVWXYZ
abcdefghijklmnopqrstuvwxyz
1234567890?!$%&
Adobe Systems, Inc.

Goudy Old Style Italic
ABCDEFGHIJKLMNOPQRSTUVWXYZ
abcdefghijklmnopqrstuvwxyz
1234567890?!$%&
Adobe Systems, Inc.

Goudy Old Style Bold
ABCDEFGHIJKLMNOPQRSTUVWXYZ
abcdefghijklmnopqrstuvwxyz
1234567890?!$%&
Adobe Systems, Inc.

Goudy Old Style Bold Italic
ABCDEFGHIJKLMNOPQRSTUVWXYZ
abcdefghijklmnopqrstuvwxyz
1234567890?!$%&
Adobe Systems, Inc.

Hancock Park

ABCDEFGHIJKLMNOPQRSTUVWXYZ
abcdefghijklmnopqrstuvwxyz
1234567890?!$%&

Dubl-Click Software, Inc.

Hancock Park Bold

ABCDEFGHIJKLMNOPQRSTUVWXYZ
abcdefghijklmnopqrstuvwxyz
1234567890?!$%&

Dubl-Click Software, Inc.

Hancock Park Light

ABCDEFGHIJKLMNOPQRSTUVWXYZ
abcdefghijklmnopqrstuvwxyz
1234567890?!$%&

Dubl-Click Software, Inc.

Helvetica 25 Ultra Light

ABCDEFGHIJKLMNOPQRSTUVWXYZ
abcdefghijklmnopqrstuvwxyz
1234567890?!$%&

Adobe Systems, Inc.

Helvetica 26 Ultra Light Italic

ABCDEFGHIJKLMNOPQRSTUVWXYZ
abcdefghijklmnopqrstuvwxyz
1234567890?!$%&

Adobe Systems, Inc.

Helvetica 35 Thin

ABCDEFGHIJKLMNOPQRSTUVWXYZ
abcdefghijklmnopqrstuvwxyz
1234567890?!$%&

Adobe Systems, Inc.

Helvetica 36 Thin Italic

ABCDEFGHIJKLMNOPQRSTUVWXYZ
abcdefghijklmnopqrstuvwxyz
1234567890?!$%&

Adobe Systems, Inc.

Helvetica 45 Light

ABCDEFGHIJKLMNOPQRSTUVWXYZ
abcdefghijklmnopqrstuvwxyz
1234567890?!$%&

Adobe Systems, Inc.

Helvetica 46 Light Italic

ABCDEFGHIJKLMNOPQRSTUVWXYZ
abcdefghijklmnopqrstuvwxyz
1234567890?!$%&

Adobe Systems, Inc.

Helvetica 55 Roman

ABCDEFGHIJKLMNOPQRSTUVWXYZ
abcdefghijklmnopqrstuvwxyz
1234567890?!$%&

Adobe Systems, Inc.

Helvetica 56 Italic

ABCDEFGHIJKLMNOPQRSTUVWXYZ
abcdefghijklmnopqrstuvwxyz
1234567890?!$%&
Adobe Systems, Inc.

Helvetica 65 Medium

ABCDEFGHIJKLMNOPQRSTUVWXYZ
abcdefghijklmnopqrstuvwxyz
1234567890?!$%&
Adobe Systems, Inc.

Helvetica 66 Medium Italic

ABCDEFGHIJKLMNOPQRSTUVWXYZ
abcdefghijklmnopqrstuvwxyz
1234567890?!$%&
Adobe Systems, Inc.

Helvetica 75 Bold

ABCDEFGHIJKLMNOPQRSTUVWXYZ
abcdefghijklmnopqrstuvwxyz
1234567890?!$%&
Adobe Systems, Inc.

Helvetica 76 Bold Italic

ABCDEFGHIJKLMNOPQRSTUVWXYZ
abcdefghijklmnopqrstuvwxyz
1234567890?!$%&
Adobe Systems, Inc.

Helvetica 85 Heavy
ABCDEFGHIJKLMNOPQRSTUVWXYZ
abcdefghijklmnopqrstuvwxyz
1234567890?!$%&
Adobe Systems, Inc.

Helvetica 86 Heavy Italic
ABCDEFGHIJKLMNOPQRSTUVWXYZ
abcdefghijklmnopqrstuvwxyz
1234567890?!$%&
Adobe Systems, Inc.

Helvetica 95 Black
ABCDEFGHIJKLMNOPQRSTUVWXYZ
abcdefghijklmnopqrstuvwxyz
1234567890?!$%&
Adobe Systems, Inc.

Helvetica 96 Black Italic
ABCDEFGHIJKLMNOPQRSTUVWXYZ
abcdefghijklmnopqrstuvwxyz
1234567890?!$%&
Adobe Systems, Inc.

Helvetica™ Black
ABCDEFGHIJKLMNOPQRSTUVWXYZ
abcdefghijklmnopqrstuvwxyz
1234567890?!$%&
Adobe Systems, Inc.

Helvetica Black Oblique
ABCDEFGHIJKLMNOPQRSTUVWXYZ
abcdefghijklmnopqrstuvwxyz
1234567890?!$%&
Adobe Systems, Inc.

Helvetica Light
ABCDEFGHIJKLMNOPQRSTUVWXYZ
abcdefghijklmnopqrstuvwxyz
1234567890?!$%&
Adobe Systems, Inc.

Helvetica Light Oblique
ABCDEFGHIJKLMNOPQRSTUVWXYZ
abcdefghijklmnopqrstuvwxyz
1234567890?!$%&
Adobe Systems, Inc.

Helvetica Condensed
ABCDEFGHIJKLMNOPQRSTUVWXYZ
abcdefghijklmnopqrstuvwxyz
1234567890?!$%&
Adobe Systems, Inc.

Helvetica Condensed Oblique
ABCDEFGHIJKLMNOPQRSTUVWXYZ
abcdefghijklmnopqrstuvwxyz
1234567890?!$%&
Adobe Systems, Inc.

Helvetica Condensed Bold
ABCDEFGHIJKLMNOPQRSTUVWXYZ
abcdefghijklmnopqrstuvwxyz
1234567890?!$%&
Adobe Systems, Inc.

Helvetica Condensed Black
ABCDEFGHIJKLMNOPQRSTUVWXYZ
abcdefghijklmnopqrstuvwxyz
1234567890?!$%&
Adobe Systems, Inc.

Helvetica Condensed Bold Oblique
ABCDEFGHIJKLMNOPQRSTUVWXYZ
abcdefghijklmnopqrstuvwxyz
1234567890?!$%&
Adobe Systems, Inc.

Helvetica Condensed Black Oblique
ABCDEFGHIJKLMNOPQRSTUVWXYZ
abcdefghijklmnopqrstuvwxyz
1234567890?!$%&
Adobe Systems, Inc.

Helvetica Condensed Light
ABCDEFGHIJKLMNOPQRSTUVWXYZ
abcdefghijklmnopqrstuvwxyz
1234567890?!$%&
Adobe Systems, Inc.

Helvetica Condensed Light Oblique
ABCDEFGHIJKLMNOPQRSTUVWXYZ
abcdefghijklmnopqrstuvwxyz
1234567890?!$%&
Adobe Systems, Inc.

Helvetica Compressed
ABCDEFGHIJKLMNOPQRSTUVWXYZ
abcdefghijklmnopqrstuvwxyz
1234567890?!$%&
Adobe Systems, Inc.

Helvetica Compressed Extra
ABCDEFGHIJKLMNOPQRSTUVWXYZ
abcdefghijklmnopqrstuvwxyz
1234567890?!$%&
Adobe Systems, Inc.

Helvetica Compressed Ultra
ABCDEFGHIJKLMNOPQRSTUVWXYZ
abcdefghijklmnopqrstuvwxyz
1234567890?!$%&
Adobe Systems, Inc.

Helvetica Inserat
ABCDEFGHIJKLMNOPQRSTUVWXYZ
abcdefghijklmnopqrstuvwxyz
1234567890?!$%&
Adobe Systems, Inc.

Hiroshige Medium
ABCDEFGHIJKLMNOPQRSTUVWXYZ
abcdefghijklmnopqrstuvwxyz
1234567890?!$%&
Adobe Systems, Inc.

Hiroshige Book
ABCDEFGHIJKLMNOPQRSTUVWXYZ
abcdefghijklmnopqrstuvwxyz
1234567890?!$%&
Adobe Systems, Inc.

Hiroshige Medium Italic
ABCDEFGHIJKLMNOPQRSTUVWXYZ
abcdefghijklmnopqrstuvwxyz
1234567890?!$%&
Adobe Systems, Inc.

Hiroshige Book Italic
ABCDEFGHIJKLMNOPQRSTUVWXYZ
abcdefghijklmnopqrstuvwxyz
1234567890?!$%&
Adobe Systems, Inc.

Hiroshige Bold
ABCDEFGHIJKLMNOPQRSTUVWXYZ
abcdefghijklmnopqrstuvwxyz
1234567890?!$%&
Adobe Systems, Inc.

Hiroshige™ Black
ABCDEFGHIJKLMNOPQRSTUVWXYZ
abcdefghijklmnopqrstuvwxyz
1234567890?!$%&
Adobe Systems, Inc.

Hiroshige Bold Italic
ABCDEFGHIJKLMNOPQRSTUVWXYZ
abcdefghijklmnopqrstuvwxyz
1234567890?!$%&
Adobe Systems, Inc.

Hiroshige Black Italic
ABCDEFGHIJKLMNOPQRSTUVWXYZ
abcdefghijklmnopqrstuvwxyz
1234567890?!$%&
Adobe Systems, Inc.

Hobo
ABCDEFGHIJKLMNOPQRSTUVWXYZ
abcdefghijklmnopqrstuvwxyz
1234567890?!$%&
Adobe Systems, Inc.

Hoboken
ABCDEFGHIJKLMNOPQRSTUVWXYZ
abcdefghijklmnopqrstuvwxyz
1234567890?!$%&
Dubl-Click Software, Inc.

Impressum
ABCDEFGHIJKLMNOPQRSTUVWXYZ
abcdefghijklmnopqrstuvwxyz
1234567890?!$%&
Agfa Corporation

Impressum Roman
ABCDEFGHIJKLMNOPQRSTUVWXYZ
abcdefghijklmnopqrstuvwxyz
1234567890?!$%&
Adobe Systems, Inc.

Impressum® Bold
ABCDEFGHIJKLMNOPQRSTUVWXYZ
abcdefghijklmnopqrstuvwxyz
1234567890?!$%&
Adobe Systems, Inc.

Impressum Bold
ABCDEFGHIJKLMNOPQRSTUVWXYZ
abcdefghijklmnopqrstuvwxyz
1234567890?!$%&
Agfa Corporation

Impressum Italic
ABCDEFGHIJKLMNOPQRSTUVWXYZ
abcdefghijklmnopqrstuvwxyz
1234567890?!$%&
Adobe Systems, Inc.

Impressum Italic
ABCDEFGHIJKLMNOPQRSTUVWXYZ
abcdefghijklmnopqrstuvwxyz
1234567890?!$%&
Agfa Corporation

Impressum Bold Italic
ABCDEFGHIJKLMNOPQRSTUVWXYZ
abcdefghijklmnopqrstuvwxyz
1234567890?!$%&
Agfa Corporation

Isabella
ABCDEFGHIJKLMNOPQRSTUVWXYZ
abcdefghijklmnopqrstuvwxyz
1234567890?!$%&
Agfa Corporation

Italia Medium
ABCDEFGHIJKLMNOPQRSTUVWXYZ
abcdefghijklmnopqrstuvwxyz
1234567890?!$%&
Adobe Systems, Inc.

Italia Book
ABCDEFGHIJKLMNOPQRSTUVWXYZ
abcdefghijklmnopqrstuvwxyz
1234567890?!$%&
Adobe Systems, Inc.

Italia Bold

ABCDEFGHIJKLMNOPQRSTUVWXYZ
abcdefghijklmnopqrstuvwxyz
1234567890?!$%&

Adobe Systems, Inc.

IXTAPA

ABCDEFGHIJKLMNOPQRSTUVWXYZ
ABCDEFGHIJKLMNOPQRSTUVWXYZ
1234567890??$%&

Dubl-Click Software, Inc.

IXTAPA BOLD

ABCDEFGHIJKLMNOPQRSTUVWXYZ
ABCDEFGHIJKLMNOPQRSTUVWXYZ
1234567890??$%&

Dubl-Click Software, Inc.

Janson Text™

ABCDEFGHIJKLMNOPQRSTUVWXYZ
abcdefghijklmnopqrstuvwxyz
1234567890?!$%&

Adobe Systems, Inc.

Janson Text Italic

ABCDEFGHIJKLMNOPQRSTUVWXYZ
abcdefghijklmnopqrstuvwxyz
1234567890?!$%&

Adobe Systems, Inc.

Janson Text Bold
ABCDEFGHIJKLMNOPQRSTUVWXYZ
abcdefghijklmnopqrstuvwxyz
1234567890?!$%&
Adobe Systems, Inc.

Janson Text Bold Italic
ABCDEFGHIJKLMNOPQRSTUVWXYZ
abcdefghijklmnopqrstuvwxyz
1234567890?!$%&
Adobe Systems, Inc.

ITC Kabel Medium
ABCDEFGHIJKLMNOPQRSTUVWXYZ
abcdefghijklmnopqrstuvwxyz
1234567890?!$%&
Adobe Systems, Inc.

ITC Kabel Book
ABCDEFGHIJKLMNOPQRSTUVWXYZ
abcdefghijklmnopqrstuvwxyz
1234567890?!$%&
Adobe Systems, Inc.

ITC Kabel® Bold
ABCDEFGHIJKLMNOPQRSTUVWXYZ
abcdefghijklmnopqrstuvwxyz
1234567890?!$%&
Adobe Systems, Inc.

ITC Kabel Demi

ABCDEFGHIJKLMNOPQRSTUVWXYZ
abcdefghijklmnopqrstuvwxyz
1234567890?!$%&

Adobe Systems, Inc.

ITC Kabel Ultra

ABCDEFGHIJKLMNOPQRSTUVWXYZ
abcdefghijklmnopqrstuvwxyz
1234567890?!$%&

Adobe Systems, Inc.

Kaufmann®

ABCDEFGHIJKLMNOPQRSTUVWXYZ
abcdefghijklmnopqrstuvwxyz
1234567890?!$%&

Adobe Systems, Inc.

Kaufmann Bold

ABCDEFGHIJKLMNOPQRSTUVWXYZ
abcdefghijklmnopqrstuvwxyz
1234567890?!$%&

Adobe Systems, Inc.

Konway Book

ABCDEFGHIJKLMNOPQRSTUVWXYZ
abcdefghijklmnopqrstuvwxyz
1234567890?!$%&

EmDash

Konway Bold

ABCDEFGHIJKLMNOPQRSTUVWXYZ
abcdefghijklmnopqrstuvwxyz
1234567890?!$%&
EmDash

Konway Heavy

ABCDEFGHIJKLMNOPQRSTUVWXYZ
abcdefghijklmnopqrstuvwxyz
1234567890?!$%&
EmDash

Konway Book Condensed

ABCDEFGHIJKLMNOPQRSTUVWXYZ
abcdefghijklmnopqrstuvwxyz
1234567890?!$%&
EmDash

Konway Bold Condensed

ABCDEFGHIJKLMNOPQRSTUVWXYZ
abcdefghijklmnopqrstuvwxyz
1234567890?!$%&
EmDash

Konway Heavy Condensed

ABCDEFGHIJKLMNOPQRSTUVWXYZ
abcdefghijklmnopqrstuvwxyz
1234567890?!$%&
EmDash

ITC Korinna Regular
ABCDEFGHIJKLMNOPQRSTUVWXYZ
abcdefghijklmnopqrstuvwxyz
1234567890?!$%&
Adobe Systems, Inc.

ITC Korinna Kursiv Regular
ABCDEFGHIJKLMNOPQRSTUVWXYZ
abcdefghijklmnopqrstuvwxyz
1234567890?!$%&
Adobe Systems, Inc.

ITC Korinna® Bold
ABCDEFGHIJKLMNOPQRSTUVWXYZ
abcdefghijklmnopqrstuvwxyz
1234567890?!$%&
Adobe Systems, Inc.

ITC Korinna Kursiv Bold
ABCDEFGHIJKLMNOPQRSTUVWXYZ
abcdefghijklmnopqrstuvwxyz
1234567890?!$%&
Adobe Systems, Inc.

SLED 16
ABCDEFGHIJKLMNOPQRSTUVWXYZ
AAABBCEFHhJKLMNPRUV°o°o!%-
1234567890? %%
Studio 231

Letter Gothic
ABCDEFGHIJKLMNOPQRSTUVWXYZ
abcdefghijklmnopqrstuvwxyz
1234567890?!$%&
Adobe Systems, Inc.

Letter Gothic Slanted
ABCDEFGHIJKLMNOPQRSTUVWXYZ
abcdefghijklmnopqrstuvwxyz
1234567890?!$%&
Adobe Systems, Inc.

Letter Gothic Bold
ABCDEFGHIJKLMNOPQRSTUVWXYZ
abcdefghijklmnopqrstuvwxyz
1234567890?!$%&
Adobe Systems, Inc.

Letter Gothic Bold Slanted
ABCDEFGHIJKLMNOPQRSTUVWXYZ
abcdefghijklmnopqrstuvwxyz
1234567890?!$%&
Adobe Systems, Inc.

Life Roman
ABCDEFGHIJKLMNOPQRSTUVWXYZ
abcdefghijklmnopqrstuvwxyz
1234567890?!$%&
Adobe Systems, Inc.

Life Italic

ABCDEFGHIJKLMNOPQRSTUVWXYZ
abcdefghijklmnopqrstuvwxyz
1234567890?!$%&
Adobe Systems, Inc.

Life® Bold

ABCDEFGHIJKLMNOPQRSTUVWXYZ
abcdefghijklmnopqrstuvwxyz
1234567890?!$%&
Adobe Systems, Inc.

Linoscript™

ABCDEFGHIJKLMNOPQRSTUVWXYZ
abcdefghijklmnopqrstuvwxyz
1234567890?!$%&
Adobe Systems, Inc.

Linotext™

ABCDEFGHIJKLMNOPQRSTUVWXYZ
abcdefghijklmnopqrstuvwxyz
1234567890?!$%&
Adobe Systems, Inc.

Linotype Centennial™ 45 Light

ABCDEFGHIJKLMNOPQRSTUVWXYZ
abcdefghijklmnopqrstuvwxyz
1234567890?!$%&
Adobe Systems, Inc.

Linotype Centennial 46 Light Italic
ABCDEFGHIJKLMNOPQRSTUVWXYZ
abcdefghijklmnopqrstuvwxyz
1234567890?!$%&
Adobe Systems, Inc.

Linotype Centennial 55
ABCDEFGHIJKLMNOPQRSTUVWXYZ
abcdefghijklmnopqrstuvwxyz
1234567890?!$%&
Adobe Systems, Inc.

Linotype Centennial 56 Italic
ABCDEFGHIJKLMNOPQRSTUVWXYZ
abcdefghijklmnopqrstuvwxyz
1234567890?!$%&
Adobe Systems, Inc.

Linotype Centennial 75 Bold
ABCDEFGHIJKLMNOPQRSTUVWXYZ
abcdefghijklmnopqrstuvwxyz
1234567890?!$%&
Adobe Systems, Inc.

Linotype Centennial 76 Bold Italic
ABCDEFGHIJKLMNOPQRSTUVWXYZ
abcdefghijklmnopqrstuvwxyz
1234567890?!$%&
Adobe Systems, Inc.

Linotype Centennial 95 Black
ABCDEFGHIJKLMNOPQRSTUVWXYZ
abcdefghijklmnopqrstuvwxyz
1234567890?!$%&
Adobe Systems, Inc.

Linotype Centennial 96 Black Italic
ABCDEFGHIJKLMNOPQRSTUVWXYZ
abcdefghijklmnopqrstuvwxyz
1234567890?!$%&
Adobe Systems, Inc.

ITC Lubalin Graph® Book
ABCDEFGHIJKLMNOPQRSTUVWXYZ
abcdefghijklmnopqrstuvwxyz
1234567890?!$%&
Adobe Systems, Inc.

ITC Lubalin Graph Book Oblique
ABCDEFGHIJKLMNOPQRSTUVWXYZ
abcdefghijklmnopqrstuvwxyz
1234567890?!$%&
Adobe Systems, Inc.

ITC Lubalin Graph Demi
ABCDEFGHIJKLMNOPQRSTUVWXYZ
abcdefghijklmnopqrstuvwxyz
1234567890?!$%&
Adobe Systems, Inc.

ITC Lubalin Graph Demi Oblique
ABCDEFGHIJKLMNOPQRSTUVWXYZ
abcdefghijklmnopqrstuvwxyz
1234567890?!$%&
Adobe Systems, Inc.

Lucida°
ABCDEFGHIJKLMNOPQRSTUVWXYZ
abcdefghijklmnopqrstuvwxyz
1234567890?!$%&
Adobe Systems, Inc.

Lucida Italic
ABCDEFGHIJKLMNOPQRSTUVWXYZ
abcdefghijklmnopqrstuvwxyz
1234567890?!$%&
Adobe Systems, Inc.

Lucida Bold
ABCDEFGHIJKLMNOPQRSTUVWXYZ
abcdefghijklmnopqrstuvwxyz
1234567890?!$%&
Adobe Systems, Inc.

Lucida Bold Italic
ABCDEFGHIJKLMNOPQRSTUVWXYZ
abcdefghijklmnopqrstuvwxyz
1234567890?!$%&
Adobe Systems, Inc.

Lucida Sans Roman
ABCDEFGHIJKLMNOPQRSTUVWXYZ
abcdefghijklmnopqrstuvwxyz
1234567890?!$%&
Adobe Systems, Inc.

Lucida Sans Italic
ABCDEFGHIJKLMNOPQRSTUVWXYZ
abcdefghijklmnopqrstuvwxyz
1234567890?!$%&
Adobe Systems, Inc.

Lucida Sans Bold
ABCDEFGHIJKLMNOPQRSTUVWXYZ
abcdefghijklmnopqrstuvwxyz
1234567890?!$%&
Adobe Systems, Inc.

Lucida Sans Bold Italic
ABCDEFGHIJKLMNOPQRSTUVWXYZ
abcdefghijklmnopqrstuvwxyz
1234567890?!$%&
Adobe Systems, Inc.

ITC MACHINE
ABCDEFGHIJKLMNOPQRSTUVWXYZ
1234567890?!$%&
Adobe Systems, Inc.

McCollough

ABCDEFGHIJKLMNOPQRSTUVWXYZ

abcdefghijklmnopqrstuvwxyz

1234567890?!$%&

Agfa Corporation

Melior™

ABCDEFGHIJKLMNOPQRSTUVWXYZ

abcdefghijklmnopqrstuvwxyz

1234567890?!$%&

Adobe Systems, Inc.

Melior Italic

ABCDEFGHIJKLMNOPQRSTUVWXYZ

abcdefghijklmnopqrstuvwxyz

1234567890?!$%&

Adobe Systems, Inc.

Melior Bold

ABCDEFGHIJKLMNOPQRSTUVWXYZ

abcdefghijklmnopqrstuvwxyz

1234567890?!$%&

Adobe Systems, Inc.

Melior Bold Italic

ABCDEFGHIJKLMNOPQRSTUVWXYZ

abcdefghijklmnopqrstuvwxyz

1234567890?!$%&

Adobe Systems, Inc.

Memphis Medium

ABCDEFGHIJKLMNOPQRSTUVWXYZ

abcdefghijklmnopqrstuvwxyz

1234567890?!$%&

Adobe Systems, Inc.

Memphis Medium Italic

ABCDEFGHIJKLMNOPQRSTUVWXYZ

abcdefghijklmnopqrstuvwxyz

1234567890?!$%&

Adobe Systems, Inc.

Memphis Bold

ABCDEFGHIJKLMNOPQRSTUVWXYZ

abcdefghijklmnopqrstuvwxyz

1234567890?!$%&

Adobe Systems, Inc.

Memphis Extra Bold

ABCDEFGHIJKLMNOPQRSTUVWXYZ

abcdefghijklmnopqrstuvwxyz

1234567890?!$%&

Adobe Systems, Inc.

Memphis Bold Italic

ABCDEFGHIJKLMNOPQRSTUVWXYZ

abcdefghijklmnopqrstuvwxyz

1234567890?!$%&

Adobe Systems, Inc.

116

Memphis Light
ABCDEFGHIJKLMNOPQRSTUVWXYZ
abcdefghijklmnopqrstuvwxyz
1234567890?!$%&
Adobe Systems, Inc.

Memphis Light Italic
ABCDEFGHIJKLMNOPQRSTUVWXYZ
abcdefghijklmnopqrstuvwxyz
1234567890?!$%&
Adobe Systems, Inc.

Méridien Bold
ABCDEFGHIJKLMNOPQRSTUVWXYZ
abcdefghijklmnopqrstuvwxyz
1234567890?!$%&
Agfa Corporation

Méridien Black
ABCDEFGHIJKLMNOPQRSTUVWXYZ
abcdefghijklmnopqrstuvwxyz
1234567890?!$%&
Agfa Corporation

Méridien Light
ABCDEFGHIJKLMNOPQRSTUVWXYZ
abcdefghijklmnopqrstuvwxyz
1234567890?!$%&
Agfa Corporation

Méridien Light Italic

ABCDEFGHIJKLMNOPQRSTUVWXYZ
abcdefghijklmnopqrstuvwxyz
1234567890?!$%&

Agfa Corporation

Metropolitan

ABCDEFGHIJKLMNOPQRSTUVWXYZ
abcdefghijklmnopqrstuvwxyz
1234567890?!$%&

Dubl-Click Software, Inc.

SMOORE COMPUTER

ABCDEFGHIJKLMNOPQRSTUVWXYZ
1234567890?!$%&

Studio 231

CGNashville Medium

ABCDEFGHIJKLMNOPQRSTUVWXYZ
abcdefghijklmnopqrstuvwxyz
1234567890?!$%&

Agfa Corporation

CGNashville Medium Italic

ABCDEFGHIJKLMNOPQRSTUVWXYZ
abcdefghijklmnopqrstuvwxyz
1234567890?!$%&

Agfa Corporation

CGNashville Bold
ABCDEFGHIJKLMNOPQRSTUVWXYZ
abcdefghijklmnopqrstuvwxyz
1234567890?!$%&
Agfa Corporation

CGNashville Bold Italic
ABCDEFGHIJKLMNOPQRSTUVWXYZ
abcdefghijklmnopqrstuvwxyz
1234567890?!$%&
Adobe Systems, Inc.

New Aster®
ABCDEFGHIJKLMNOPQRSTUVWXYZ
abcdefghijklmnopqrstuvwxyz
1234567890?!$%&
Adobe Systems, Inc.

New Aster Italic
ABCDEFGHIJKLMNOPQRSTUVWXYZ
abcdefghijklmnopqrstuvwxyz
1234567890?!$%&
Adobe Systems, Inc.

New Aster Bold
ABCDEFGHIJKLMNOPQRSTUVWXYZ
abcdefghijklmnopqrstuvwxyz
1234567890?!$%&
Adobe Systems, Inc.

New Aster Black
ABCDEFGHIJKLMNOPQRSTUVWXYZ
abcdefghijklmnopqrstuvwxyz
1234567890?!$%&
Adobe Systems, Inc.

New Aster Semibold
ABCDEFGHIJKLMNOPQRSTUVWXYZ
abcdefghijklmnopqrstuvwxyz
1234567890?!$%&
Adobe Systems, Inc.

New Aster Bold Italic
ABCDEFGHIJKLMNOPQRSTUVWXYZ
abcdefghijklmnopqrstuvwxyz
1234567890?!$%&
Adobe Systems, Inc.

New Aster Black Italic
ABCDEFGHIJKLMNOPQRSTUVWXYZ
abcdefghijklmnopqrstuvwxyz
1234567890?!$%&
Adobe Systems, Inc.

New Aster Semibold Italic
ABCDEFGHIJKLMNOPQRSTUVWXYZ
abcdefghijklmnopqrstuvwxyz
1234567890?!$%&
Adobe Systems, Inc.

ITC New Baskerville Roman
ABCDEFGHIJKLMNOPQRSTUVWXYZ
abcdefghijklmnopqrstuvwxyz
1234567890?!$%&
Adobe Systems, Inc.

ITC New Baskerville Italic
ABCDEFGHIJKLMNOPQRSTUVWXYZ
abcdefghijklmnopqrstuvwxyz
1234567890?!$%&
Adobe Systems, Inc.

ITC New Baskerville® Bold
ABCDEFGHIJKLMNOPQRSTUVWXYZ
abcdefghijklmnopqrstuvwxyz
1234567890?!$%&
Adobe Systems, Inc.

ITC New Baskerville Bold Italic
ABCDEFGHIJKLMNOPQRSTUVWXYZ
abcdefghijklmnopqrstuvwxyz
1234567890?!$%&
Adobe Systems, Inc.

New Caledonia™
ABCDEFGHIJKLMNOPQRSTUVWXYZ
abcdefghijklmnopqrstuvwxyz
1234567890?!$%&
Adobe Systems, Inc.

New Caledonia Italic

ABCDEFGHIJKLMNOPQRSTUVWXYZ
abcdefghijklmnopqrstuvwxyz
1234567890?!$%&
Adobe Systems, Inc.

New Caledonia Bold

ABCDEFGHIJKLMNOPQRSTUVWXYZ
abcdefghijklmnopqrstuvwxyz
1234567890?!$%&
Adobe Systems, Inc.

New Caledonia Black

ABCDEFGHIJKLMNOPQRSTUVWXYZ
abcdefghijklmnopqrstuvwxyz
1234567890?!$%&
Adobe Systems, Inc.

New Caledonia Semi Bold

ABCDEFGHIJKLMNOPQRSTUVWXYZ
abcdefghijklmnopqrstuvwxyz
1234567890?!$%&
Adobe Systems, Inc.

New Caledonia Bold Italic

ABCDEFGHIJKLMNOPQRSTUVWXYZ
abcdefghijklmnopqrstuvwxyz
1234567890?!$%&
Adobe Systems, Inc.

New Caledonia Black Italic
ABCDEFGHIJKLMNOPQRSTUVWXYZ
abcdefghijklmnopqrstuvwxyz
1234567890?!$%&
Adobe Systems, Inc.

New Caledonia Semi Bold Italic
ABCDEFGHIJKLMNOPQRSTUVWXYZ
abcdefghijklmnopqrstuvwxyz
1234567890?!$%&
Adobe Systems, Inc.

New Century Schoolbook
ABCDEFGHIJKLMNOPQRSTUVWXYZ
abcdefghijklmnopqrstuvwxyz
1234567890?!$%&
Adobe Systems, Inc.

New Century Schoolbook Italic
ABCDEFGHIJKLMNOPQRSTUVWXYZ
abcdefghijklmnopqrstuvwxyz
1234567890?!$%&
Adobe Systems, Inc.

New Century Schoolbook Bold
ABCDEFGHIJKLMNOPQRSTUVWXYZ
abcdefghijklmnopqrstuvwxyz
1234567890?!$%&
Adobe Systems, Inc.

New Century Schoolbook Bold Italic
ABCDEFGHIJKLMNOPQRSTUVWXYZ
abcdefghijklmnopqrstuvwxyz
1234567890?!$%&
Adobe Systems, Inc.

News Gothic
ABCDEFGHIJKLMNOPQRSTUVWXYZ
abcdefghijklmnopqrstuvwxyz
1234567890?!$%&
Adobe Systems, Inc.

News Gothic Oblique
ABCDEFGHIJKLMNOPQRSTUVWXYZ
abcdefghijklmnopqrstuvwxyz
1234567890?!$%&
Adobe Systems, Inc.

News Gothic Bold
ABCDEFGHIJKLMNOPQRSTUVWXYZ
abcdefghijklmnopqrstuvwxyz
1234567890?!$%&
Adobe Systems, Inc.

News Gothic Bold Oblique
ABCDEFGHIJKLMNOPQRSTUVWXYZ
abcdefghijklmnopqrstuvwxyz
1234567890?!$%&
Agfa Corporation

ITC Novarese Book

ABCDEFGHIJKLMNOPQRSTUVWXYZ
abcdefghijklmnopqrstuvwxyz
1234567890?!$%&

Agfa Corporation

ITC *Novarese Book Italic*

ABCDEFGHIJKLMNOPQRSTUVWXYZ
abcdefghijklmnopqrstuvwxyz
1234567890?!$%&

Agfa Corporation

ITC Novarese Bold

ABCDEFGHIJKLMNOPQRSTUVWXYZ
abcdefghijklmnopqrstuvwxyz
1234567890?!$%&

Agfa Corporation

ITC *Novarese Bold Italic*

ABCDEFGHIJKLMNOPQRSTUVWXYZ
abcdefghijklmnopqrstuvwxyz
1234567890?!$%&

Agfa Corporation

OCR A

ABCDEFGHIJKLMNOPQRSTUVWXYZ
abcdefghijklmnopqrstuvwxyz
1234567890?!$%&

Adobe Systems, Inc.

OCRB

ABCDEFGHIJKLMNOPQRSTUVWXYZ
abcdefghijklmnopqrstuvwxyz
1234567890?!$%&

Adobe Systems, Inc.

Optima™

ABCDEFGHIJKLMNOPQRSTUVWXYZ
abcdefghijklmnopqrstuvwxyz
1234567890?!$%&

Adobe Systems, Inc.

Optima Oblique

ABCDEFGHIJKLMNOPQRSTUVWXYZ
abcdefghijklmnopqrstuvwxyz
1234567890?!$%&

Adobe Systems, Inc.

Optima Bold

ABCDEFGHIJKLMNOPQRSTUVWXYZ
abcdefghijklmnopqrstuvwxyz
1234567890?!$%&

Adobe Systems, Inc.

Optima Bold Oblique

ABCDEFGHIJKLMNOPQRSTUVWXYZ
abcdefghijklmnopqrstuvwxyz
1234567890?!$%&

Adobe Systems, Inc.

ORATOR

ABCDEFGHIJKLMNOPQRSTUVWXYZ
ABCDEFGHIJKLMNOPQRSTUVWXYZ
1234567890?!$%&
Adobe Systems, Inc.

ORATOR SLANTED

ABCDEFGHIJKLMNOPQRSTUVWXYZ
ABCDEFGHIJKLMNOPQRSTUVWXYZ
1234567890?!$%&
Adobe Systems, Inc.

Palatino™

ABCDEFGHIJKLMNOPQRSTUVWXYZ
abcdefghijklmnopqrstuvwxyz
1234567890?!$%&
Adobe Systems, Inc.

Palatino Italic

ABCDEFGHIJKLMNOPQRSTUVWXYZ
abcdefghijklmnopqrstuvwxyz
1234567890?!$%&
Adobe Systems, Inc.

Palatino Bold

ABCDEFGHIJKLMNOPQRSTUVWXYZ
abcdefghijklmnopqrstuvwxyz
1234567890?!$%&
Adobe Systems, Inc.

127

Palatino Bold Italic
ABCDEFGHIJKLMNOPQRSTUVWXYZ
abcdefghijklmnopqrstuvwxyz
1234567890?!$%&
Adobe Systems, Inc.

PALOMAR™ Bold
ABCDEFGHIJKLMNOPQRSTUVWXYZ
abcdefghijklmnopqrstuvwxyz
1234567890?!$%&
EmDash

Park Avenue®
ABCDEFGHIJKLMNOPQRSTUVWXYZ
abcdefghijklmnopqrstuvwxyz
1234567890?!$%&
Adobe Systems, Inc.

Peignot™ Bold
ABCDEFGHIJKLMNOPQRSTUVWXYZ
abcdefghijklmnopqrstuvwxyz
1234567890?!$%&
Adobe Systems, Inc.

Peignot Demi
ABCDEFGHIJKLMNOPQRSTUVWXYZ
abcdefghijklmnopqrstuvwxyz
1234567890?!$%&
Adobe Systems, Inc.

Peignot Light

ABCDEFGHIJKLMNOPQRSTUVWXYZ

abcdefghijklmnopqrstuvwxyz

1234567890?!$%&

Adobe Systems, Inc.

SDOUBLE PIPE

ABCDEFGHIJKLMNOPQRSTUVWXYZ

1234567890?!$%&

Studio 231

SSINGLE PIPE

ABCDEFGHIJKLMNOPQRSTUVWXYZ

1234567890?!$%&

Studio 231

Plymouth

ABCDEFGHIJKLMNOPQRSTUVWXYZ

abcdefghijklmnopqrstuvwxyz

1234567890?!$%&

T/Maker

Plymouth Gray

ABCDEFGHIJKLMNOPQRSTUVWXYZ

abcdefghijklmnopqrstuvwxyz

1234567890?!$%&

T/Maker

Post Antiqua™

ABCDEFGHIJKLMNOPQRSTUVWXYZ

abcdefghijklmnopqrstuvwxyz

1234567890!!$%&

Adobe Systems, Inc.

Post Antiqua Bold

ABCDEFGHIJKLMNOPQRSTUVWXYZ

abcdefghijklmnopqrstuvwxyz

1234567890!!$%&

Adobe Systems, Inc.

Present™ Script

ABCDEFGHIJKLMNOPQRSTUVWXYZ

abcdefghijklmnopqrstuvwxyz

1234567890?!$%&

Adobe Systems, Inc.

Prestige Elite

ABCDEFGHIJKLMNOPQRSTUVWXYZ

abcdefghijklmnopqrstuvwxyz

1234567890?!$%&

Adobe Systems, Inc.

Prestige Elite Slanted

ABCDEFGHIJKLMNOPQRSTUVWXYZ

abcdefghijklmnopqrstuvwxyz

1234567890?!$%&

Adobe Systems, Inc.

Prestige Elite Bold
ABCDEFGHIJKLMNOPQRSTUVWXYZ
abcdefghijklmnopqrstuvwxyz
1234567890?!$%&
Adobe Systems, Inc.

Prestige Elite Bold Slanted
ABCDEFGHIJKLMNOPQRSTUVWXYZ
abcdefghijklmnopqrstuvwxyz
1234567890?!$%&
Adobe Systems, Inc.

Prospera
ABCDEFGHIJKLMNOPQRSTUVWXYZ
abcdefghijklmnopqrstuvwxyz
1234567890?!$%&
Alphabets, Inc.

Raleigh Medium
ABCDEFGHIJKLMNOPQRSTUVWXYZ
abcdefghijklmnopqrstuvwxyz
1234567890?!$%&
Agfa Corporation

Raleigh Bold
ABCDEFGHIJKLMNOPQRSTUVWXYZ
abcdefghijklmnopqrstuvwxyz
1234567890?!$%&
Agfa Corporation

Raleigh Extra Bold

ABCDEFGHIJKLMNOPQRSTUVWXYZ
abcdefghijklmnopqrstuvwxyz
1234567890?!$%&

Agfa Corporation

Raleigh Light

ABCDEFGHIJKLMNOPQRSTUVWXYZ
abcdefghijklmnopqrstuvwxyz
1234567890?!$%&

Agfa Corporation

Raphael

ABCDEFGHIJKLMNOPQRSTUVWXYZ
abcdefghijklmnopqrstuvwxyz
1234567890?!$%&

Agfa Corporation

Revue

ABCDEFGHIJKLMNOPQRSTUVWXYZ
abcdefghijklmnopqrstuvwxyz
1234567890?!$%&

Adobe Systems, Inc.

SRevue

ABCDEFGHIJKLMNOPQRSTUVWXYZ
abcdefghijklmnopqrstuvwxyz
1234567890?!$%&

Studio 231

SRICCARDO
ABCDEFGHIJKLMNOPQRSTUVWXYZ
1234567890?!$%&
Studio 231

SRound Black
ABCDEFGHIJKLMNOPQRSTUVWXYZ
abcdefghijklmnopqrstuvwxyz
1234567890?!$%&
Studio 231

SRussell Square
ABCDEFGHIJKLMNOPQRSTUVWXYZ
abcdefghijklmnopqrstuvwxyz
1234567890?!$%&
Studio 231

SRussell Square Italic
ABCDEFGHIJKLMNOPQRSTUVWXY
Zabcdefghijklmnopqrstuvwxyz
1234567890?!$%&
Studio 231

SRussell Square Bold
ABCDEFGHIJKLMNOPQRSTUVWXYZ
abcdefghijklmnopqrstuvwxyz
1234567890?!$%&
Studio 231

SRussell Square Extra Bold
ABCDEFGHIJKLMNOPQRSTUVWXYZ
abcdefghijklmnopqrstuvwxyz
1234567890?!$%&
Studio 231

SRussell Square Light
ABCDEFGHIJKLMNOPQRSTUVWXYZ
abcdefghijklmnopqrstuvwxyz
1234567890?!$%&
Studio 231

SRussell Square Extra Light
ABCDEFGHIJKLMNOPQRSTUVWXYZ
abcdefghijklmnopqrstuvwxyz
1234567890?!$%&
Studio 231

SRussell Square Light Italic
ABCDEFGHIJKLMNOPQRSTUVWX
YZabcdefghijklmnopqrstuvwxyz
1234567890?!$%&
Studio 231

SRussell Square Extra Light Italic
ABCDEFGHIJKLMNOPQRSTUVWX
YZabcdefghijklmnopqrstuvwxyz
1234567890?!$%&
Studio 231

Sabon™

ABCDEFGHIJKLMNOPQRSTUVWXYZ
abcdefghijklmnopqrstuvwxyz
1234567890?!$%&
Adobe Systems, Inc.

Sabon Italic

ABCDEFGHIJKLMNOPQRSTUVWXYZ
abcdefghijklmnopqrstuvwxyz
1234567890?!$%&
Adobe Systems, Inc.

Sabon Bold

ABCDEFGHIJKLMNOPQRSTUVWXYZ
abcdefghijklmnopqrstuvwxyz
1234567890?!$%&
Adobe Systems, Inc.

Sabon Bold Italic

ABCDEFGHIJKLMNOPQRSTUVWXYZ
abcdefghijklmnopqrstuvwxyz
1234567890?!$%&
Adobe Systems, Inc.

Saigon

ABCDEFGHIJKLMNOPQRSTUVWXYZ
abcdefghijklmnopqrstuvwxyz
1234567890?!$%&
Dubl-Click Software, Inc.

Santa Monica
ABCDEFGHIJKLMNOPQRSTUVWXYZ
abcdefghijklmnopqrstuvwxyz
1234567890?!$%&
Dubl-Click Software, Inc.

Santa Monica Bold
ABCDEFGHIJKLMNOPQRSTUVWXYZ
abcdefghijklmnopqrstuvwxyz
1234567890?!$%&
Dubl-Click Software, Inc.

Santa Monica Ultra
ABCDEFGHIJKLMNOPQRSTUVWXYZ
abcdefghijklmnopqrstuvwxyz
1234567890?!$%&
Dubl-Click Software, Inc.

Schneidler
ABCDEFGHIJKLMNOPQRSTUVWXYZ
abcdefghijklmnopqrstuvwxyz
1234567890?!$%&
Agfa Corporation

Schneidler Italic
ABCDEFGHIJKLMNOPQRSTUVWXYZ
abcdefghijklmnopqrstuvwxyz
1234567890?!$%&
Agfa Corporation

Schneidler Bold
ABCDEFGHIJKLMNOPQRSTUVWXYZ
abcdefghijklmnopqrstuvwxyz
1234567890?!$%&
Agfa Corporation

Schneidler Bold Italic
ABCDEFGHIJKLMNOPQRSTUVWXYZ
abcdefghijklmnopqrstuvwxyz
1234567890?!$%&
Agfa Corporation

ITC Serif Gothic®
ABCDEFGHIJKLMNOPQRSTUVWXYZ
abcdefghijklmnopqrstuvwxyz
1234567890?!$%&
Adobe Systems, Inc.

ITC Serif Gothic Bold
ABCDEFGHIJKLMNOPQRSTUVWXYZ
abcdefghijklmnopqrstuvwxyz
1234567890?!$%&
Adobe Systems, Inc.

ITC Serif Gothic Extra Bold
ABCDEFGHIJKLMNOPQRSTUVWXYZ
abcdefghijklmnopqrstuvwxyz
1234567890?!$%&
Adobe Systems, Inc.

ITC Serif Gothic Black
ABCDEFGHIJKLMNOPQRSTUVWXYZ
abcdefghijklmnopqrstuvwxyz
1234567890?!$%&
Adobe Systems, Inc.

ITC Serif Gothic Heavy
ABCDEFGHIJKLMNOPQRSTUVWXYZ
abcdefghijklmnopqrstuvwxyz
1234567890?!$%&
Adobe Systems, Inc.

ITC Serif Gothic Light
ABCDEFGHIJKLMNOPQRSTUVWXYZ
abcdefghijklmnopqrstuvwxyz
1234567890?!$%&
Adobe Systems, Inc.

Serifa® 45 Light
ABCDEFGHIJKLMNOPQRSTUVWXYZ
abcdefghijklmnopqrstuvwxyz
1234567890?!$%&
Adobe Systems, Inc.

Serifa 46 Light Italic
ABCDEFGHIJKLMNOPQRSTUVWXYZ
abcdefghijklmnopqrstuvwxyz
1234567890?!$%&
Adobe Systems, Inc.

138

Serifa 55

ABCDEFGHIJKLMNOPQRSTUVWXYZ
abcdefghijklmnopqrstuvwxyz
1234567890?!$%&
Adobe Systems, Inc.

Serifa 56 Italic

ABCDEFGHIJKLMNOPQRSTUVWXYZ
abcdefghijklmnopqrstuvwxyz
1234567890?!$%&
Adobe Systems, Inc.

Serifa 65 Bold

ABCDEFGHIJKLMNOPQRSTUVWXYZ
abcdefghijklmnopqrstuvwxyz
1234567890?!$%&
Adobe Systems, Inc.

Serifa 75 Black

ABCDEFGHIJKLMNOPQRSTUVWXYZ
abcdefghijklmnopqrstuvwxyz
1234567890?!$%&
Adobe Systems, Inc.

SSerpentine Medium

ABCDEFGHIJKLMNOPQRSTUVWX
YZabcdefghIJklmnopqrstuvwxy
z1234567890?!$%&
Studio 231

SSerpentine Bold
ABCDEFGHIJKLMNOPQRSTUV
WXYZabcdefghijklmnopqrst
uvwxyz1234567890?!$%&

Studio 231

SSerpentine Bold Italic
ABCDEFGHIJKLMNOPQRST
UVWXYZabcdefghijklmno
pqrstuvwxyz1234567890?
!$%&

Studio 231

SSerpentine Light
ABCDEFGHIJKLMNOPQRSTUVWXYZ
abcdefghijklmnopqrstuvwxyz
1234567890?!$%&

Studio 231

Seville
ABCDEFGHIJKLMNOPQRSTUVWXYZ
abcdefghijklmnopqrstuvwxyz
1234567890?!$%&

T/Maker

Seville Gray
ABCDEFGHIJKLMNOPQRSTUVWXYZ
abcdefghijklmnopqrstuvwxyz
1234567890?!$%&

T/Maker

Shannon Book

ABCDEFGHIJKLMNOPQRSTUVWXYZ
abcdefghijklmnopqrstuvwxyz
1234567890?!$%&

Agfa Corporation

Shannon Oblique

ABCDEFGHIJKLMNOPQRSTUVWXYZ
abcdefghijklmnopqrstuvwxyz
1234567890?!$%&

Agfa Corporation

Shannon Bold

ABCDEFGHIJKLMNOPQRSTUVWXYZ
abcdefghijklmnopqrstuvwxyz
1234567890?!$%&

Agfa Corporation

Shannon Extrabold

ABCDEFGHIJKLMNOPQRSTUVWXYZ
abcdefghijklmnopqrstuvwxyz
1234567890?!$%&

Agfa Corporation

ITC Souvenir®

ABCDEFGHIJKLMNOPQRSTUVWXYZ
abcdefghijklmnopqrstuvwxyz
1234567890?!$%&

Adobe Systems, Inc.

ITC Souvenir Demi

ABCDEFGHIJKLMNOPQRSTUVWXYZ
abcdefghijklmnopqrstuvwxyz
1234567890?!$%&

Adobe Systems, Inc.

ITC Souvenir Demi Italic

ABCDEFGHIJKLMNOPQRSTUVWXYZ
abcdefghijklmnopqrstuvwxyz
1234567890?!$%&

Adobe Systems, Inc.

ITC Souvenir Light Italic

ABCDEFGHIJKLMNOPQRSTUVWXYZ
abcdefghijklmnopqrstuvwxyz
1234567890?!$%&

Adobe Systems, Inc.

sstan Free

ABCDEFGHIJKLMNOPQRSTUVW
XYZabcdefghijklmnopqrstuvw
XYZ1234567890?!$%&

Studio 231

SStandard

ABCDEFGHIJKLMNOPQRSTUVWXYZ
abcdefghijklmnopqrstuvwxyz
1234567890?!$%&

Studio 231

SStandard Medium
ABCDEFGHIJKLMNOPQRSTUVWXYZ
abcdefghijklmnopqrstuvwxyz
1234567890?!$%&
Studio 231

SStandard Bold
ABCDEFGHIJKLMNOPQRSTUVWXYZ
abcdefghijklmnopqrstuvwxyz
1234567890?!$%&
Studio 231

SStandard Light
ABCDEFGHIJKLMNOPQRSTUVWXYZ
abcdefghijklmnopqrstuvwxyz
1234567890?!$%&
Studio 231

SStandard Condensed
ABCDEFGHIJKLMNOPQRSTUVWXYZ
abcdefghijklmnopqrstuvwxyz
1234567890?!$%&
Studio 231

SStandard Medium Condensed
ABCDEFGHIJKLMNOPQRSTUVWXYZ
abcdefghijklmnopqrstuvwxyz
1234567890?!$%&
Studio 231

SStandard Bold Condensed
ABCDEFGHIJKLMNOPQRSTUVWXYZ
abcdefghijklmnopqrstuvwxyz
1234567890?!$%&
Studio 231

SStandard Extra Bold Condensed
ABCDEFGHIJKLMNOPQRSTUVWXYZ
abcdefghijklmnopqrstuvwxyz
1234567890?!$%&
Studio 231

SStandard Extended
ABCDEFGHIJKLMNOPQRSTUVW
XYZabcdefghijklmnopqrstuvwxyz
1234567890?!$%&
Studio 231

SStd. Extra Bold Extended
ABCDEFGHIJKLMNOPQRSTU
VWXYabcdefghijklmnopqrst
uvwxyz1234567890?!$%&
Studio 231

SStandard Light Extended
ABCDEFGHIJKLMNOPQRSTUVW
XYZabcdefghijklmnopqrstuvwxyz
1234567890?!$%&
Studio 231

SStandard Extra Light Extended
ABCDEFGHIJKLMNOPQRSTUVWX YZabcdefghijklmnopqrstuvwxyz 1234567890?!$%&
Studio 231

SStark Debonair
ABCDEFGHIJKLMNOPQRSTUVWXYZ abcdefghijklmnopqrstuvwxyz 1234567890?!$%&
Studio 231

SStark Debonair Mono Bold
ABCDEFGHIJKLMNOPQRSTUVWXYZ abcdefghijklmnopqrstuvwxyz 1234567890?!$%&
Studio 231

SStark Debonair Semi Bold
ABCDEFGHIJKLMNOPQRSTUVWXYZ abcdefghijklmnopqrstuvwxyz 1234567890?!$%&
Studio 231

SSTEELPLATE GOTHIC BOLD
ABCDEFGHIJKLMNOPQRSTUV WXYZ1234567890?!$%&
Studio 231

STENCIL
ABCDEFGHIJKLMNOPQRSTUVWXYZ
1234567890?!$%&
Adobe Systems, Inc.

Stone® Informal
ABCDEFGHIJKLMNOPQRSTUVWXYZ
abcdefghijklmnopqrstuvwxyz
1234567890?!$%&
Adobe Systems, Inc.

Stone Informal Italic
ABCDEFGHIJKLMNOPQRSTUVWXYZ
abcdefghijklmnopqrstuvwxyz
1234567890?!$%&
Adobe Systems, Inc.

Stone Informal Bold
ABCDEFGHIJKLMNOPQRSTUVWXYZ
abcdefghijklmnopqrstuvwxyz
1234567890?!$%&
Adobe Systems, Inc.

Stone Informal Semibold
ABCDEFGHIJKLMNOPQRSTUVWXYZ
abcdefghijklmnopqrstuvwxyz
1234567890?!$%&
Adobe Systems, Inc.

Stone Informal Bold Italic
ABCDEFGHIJKLMNOPQRSTUVWXYZ
abcdefghijklmnopqrstuvwxyz
1234567890?!$%&
Adobe Systems, Inc.

Stone Informal Semibold Italic
ABCDEFGHIJKLMNOPQRSTUVWXYZ
abcdefghijklmnopqrstuvwxyz
1234567890?!$%&
Adobe Systems, Inc.

Stone Sans
ABCDEFGHIJKLMNOPQRSTUVWXYZ
abcdefghijklmnopqrstuvwxyz
1234567890?!$%&
Adobe Systems, Inc.

Stone Sans Italic
ABCDEFGHIJKLMNOPQRSTUVWXYZ
abcdefghijklmnopqrstuvwxyz
1234567890?!$%&
Adobe Systems, Inc.

Stone Sans Bold
ABCDEFGHIJKLMNOPQRSTUVWXYZ
abcdefghijklmnopqrstuvwxyz
1234567890?!$%&
Adobe Systems, Inc.

Stone Sans Semibold
ABCDEFGHIJKLMNOPQRSTUVWXYZ
abcdefghijklmnopqrstuvwxyz
1234567890?!$%&
Adobe Systems, Inc.

Stone Sans Bold Italic
ABCDEFGHIJKLMNOPQRSTUVWXYZ
abcdefghijklmnopqrstuvwxyz
1234567890?!$%&
Adobe Systems, Inc.

Stone Sans Semibold Italic
ABCDEFGHIJKLMNOPQRSTUVWXYZ
abcdefghijklmnopqrstuvwxyz
1234567890?!$%&
Adobe Systems, Inc.

Stone Serif
ABCDEFGHIJKLMNOPQRSTUVWXYZ
abcdefghijklmnopqrstuvwxyz
1234567890?!$%&
Adobe Systems, Inc.

Stone Serif Italic
ABCDEFGHIJKLMNOPQRSTUVWXYZ
abcdefghijklmnopqrstuvwxyz
1234567890?!$%&
Adobe Systems, Inc.

Stone Serif Bold
ABCDEFGHIJKLMNOPQRSTUVWXYZ
abcdefghijklmnopqrstuvwxyz
1234567890?!$%&
Adobe Systems, Inc.

Stone Serif Semibold
ABCDEFGHIJKLMNOPQRSTUVWXYZ
abcdefghijklmnopqrstuvwxyz
1234567890?!$%&
Adobe Systems, Inc.

Stone Serif Bold Italic
ABCDEFGHIJKLMNOPQRSTUVWXYZ
abcdefghijklmnopqrstuvwxyz
1234567890?!$%&
Adobe Systems, Inc.

Stone Serif Semibold Italic
ABCDEFGHIJKLMNOPQRSTUVWXYZ
abcdefghijklmnopqrstuvwxyz
1234567890?!$%&
Adobe Systems, Inc.

CG Symphony
ABCDEFGHIJKLMNOPQRSTUVWXYZ
abcdefghijklmnopqrstuvwxyz
1234567890?!$%&
Adobe Systems, Inc.

CG Symphony Italic

ABCDEFGHIJKLMNOPQRSTUVWXYZ
abcdefghijklmnopqrstuvwxyz
1234567890?!$%&

Adobe Systems, Inc.

CG Symphony Bold

ABCDEFGHIJKLMNOPQRSTUVWXYZ
abcdefghijklmnopqrstuvwxyz
1234567890?!$%&

Agfa Corporation

CG Symphony Black

ABCDEFGHIJKLMNOPQRSTUVWXYZ
abcdefghijklmnopqrstuvwxyz
1234567890?!$%&

Agfa Corporation

SSyntax

ABCDEFGHIJKLMNOPQRSTUVWXYZ
abcdefghijklmnopqrstuvwxyz
1234567890?!$%&

Studio 231

SSyntax Bold

ABCDEFGHIJKLMNOPQRSTUVWXYZ
abcdefghijklmnopqrstuvwxyz
1234567890?!$%&

Studio 231

SSyntax Ultra Bold
ABCDEFGHIJKLMNOPQRSTUVWX
YZabcdefghijklmnopqrstuvwxyz
1234567890?!$%&
Studio 231

ST.H.ALPHABET SOUP
ABCDEFGHIJKLMNOPQRSTUVWXYZ
1234567890?!$%&
Studio 231

STango
ABCDEFGHIJKLMNOPQRSTUVW
XYZabcdefghijklmnopqrstuvwxyz
1234567890?!$%&
Studio 231

Tempo Heavy Condensed
ABCDEFGHIJKLMNOPQRSTUVWXYZ
abcdefghijklmnopqrstuvwxyz
1234567890?!$%&
Adobe Systems, Inc.

Tempo Heavy Condensed Italic
ABCDEFGHIJKLMNOPQRSTUVWXYZ
abcdefghijklmnopqrstuvwxyz
1234567890?!$%&
Adobe Systems, Inc.

151

SThorowgood Roman
ABCDEFGHIJKLMNOPQRSTU VWXYZabcdefghijklmnopqrst uvwxyz1234567890?!$%&
Studio 231

SThorowgood Italic
ABCDEFGHIJKLMNOPQ RSTUVWXYZabcdefghijkl mnopqrstuvwxyz123456789 0?!$%&
Studio 231

SThreshold
ABCDEFGHIJKLMNOPQRSTUVWXYZ abcdefghijklmnopqrstuvwxyz 1234567890?!$%&
Studio 231

STHUNDERBIRD EXTRA CONDENSED
ABCDEFGHIJKLMNOPQRSTUVWXYZ 1234567890?!$%&
Studio 231

ITC Tiffany®
ABCDEFGHIJKLMNOPQRSTUVWXYZ abcdefghijklmnopqrstuvwxyz 1234567890?!$%&
Adobe Systems, Inc.

152

ITC Tiffany Italic
ABCDEFGHIJKLMNOPQRSTUVWXYZ
abcdefghijklmnopqrstuvwxyz
1234567890?!$%&
Adobe Systems, Inc.

ITC Tiffany Demi
ABCDEFGHIJKLMNOPQRSTUVWXYZ
abcdefghijklmnopqrstuvwxyz
1234567890?!$%&
Adobe Systems, Inc.

ITC Tiffany Heavy
ABCDEFGHIJKLMNOPQRSTUVWXYZ
abcdefghijklmnopqrstuvwxyz
1234567890?!$%&
Adobe Systems, Inc.

ITC Tiffany Demi Italic
ABCDEFGHIJKLMNOPQRSTUVWXYZ
abcdefghijklmnopqrstuvwxyz
1234567890?!$%&
Adobe Systems, Inc.

ITC Tiffany Heavy Italic
ABCDEFGHIJKLMNOPQRSTUVWXY
Zabcdefghijklmnopqrstuvwxyz
1234567890?!$%&
Adobe Systems, Inc.

153

Times Ten Roman

ABCDEFGHIJKLMNOPQRSTUVWXYZ
abcdefghijklmnopqrstuvwxyz
1234567890?!$%&

Adobe Systems, Inc.

Times Ten Italic

ABCDEFGHIJKLMNOPQRSTUVWXYZ
abcdefghijklmnopqrstuvwxyz
1234567890?!$%&

Adobe Systems, Inc.

Times™ Ten Bold

ABCDEFGHIJKLMNOPQRSTUVWXYZ
abcdefghijklmnopqrstuvwxyz
1234567890?!$%&

Adobe Systems, Inc.

Times Ten Bold Italic

ABCDEFGHIJKLMNOPQRSTUVWXYZ
abcdefghijklmnopqrstuvwxyz
1234567890?!$%&

Adobe Systems, Inc.

CG Triumvirate

ABCDEFGHIJKLMNOPQRSTUVWXYZ
abcdefghijklmnopqrstuvwxyz
1234567890?!$%&

Agfa Corporation

CG Triumvirate Italic
ABCDEFGHIJKLMNOPQRSTUVWXYZ
abcdefghijklmnopqrstuvwxyz
1234567890?!$%&
Agfa Corporation

CG Triumvirate Bold
ABCDEFGHIJKLMNOPQRSTUVWXYZ
abcdefghijklmnopqrstuvwxyz
1234567890?!$%&
Agfa Corporation

CG Triumvirate Bold Italic
ABCDEFGHIJKLMNOPQRSTUVWXYZ
abcdefghijklmnopqrstuvwxyz
1234567890?!$%&
Agfa Corporation

CG Triumvirate Inserat
ABCDEFGHIJKLMNOPQRSTUVWXYZ
abcdefghijklmnopqrstuvwxyz
1234567890?!$%&
Agfa Corporation

CG Triumvirate Inserat Italic
ABCDEFGHIJKLMNOPQRSTUVWXYZ
abcdefghijklmnopqrstuvwxyz
1234567890?!$%&
Agfa Corporation

CG Triumvirate Compressed
ABCDEFGHIJKLMNOPQRSTUVWXYZ
abcdefghijklmnopqrstuvwxyz
1234567890?!$%&
Agfa Corporation

CG Triumvirate Extra Compressed
ABCDEFGHIJKLMNOPQRSTUVWXYZ
abcdefghijklmnopqrstuvwxyz
1234567890?!$%&
Agfa Corporation

Trump Mediaeval™
ABCDEFGHIJKLMNOPQRSTUVWXYZ
abcdefghijklmnopqrstuvwxyz
1234567890?!$%&
Adobe Systems, Inc.

Trump Mediaeval Italic
ABCDEFGHIJKLMNOPQRSTUVWXYZ
abcdefghijklmnopqrstuvwxyz
1234567890?!$%&
Adobe Systems, Inc.

Trump Mediaeval Bold
ABCDEFGHIJKLMNOPQRSTUVWXYZ
abcdefghijklmnopqrstuvwxyz
1234567890?!$%&
Adobe Systems, Inc.

Trump Mediaeval Bold Italic
ABCDEFGHIJKLMNOPQRSTUVWXYZ
abcdefghijklmnopqrstuvwxyz
1234567890?!$%&
Adobe Systems, Inc.

CG Trump Mediaeval
ABCDEFGHIJKLMNOPQRSTUVWXYZ
abcdefghijklmnopqrstuvwxyz
1234567890?!$%&
Agfa Corporation

CG Trump Mediaeval Italic
ABCDEFGHIJKLMNOPQRSTUVWXYZ
abcdefghijklmnopqrstuvwxyz
1234567890?!$%&
Agfa Corporation

CG Trump Mediaeval Bold
ABCDEFGHIJKLMNOPQRSTUVWXYZ
abcdefghijklmnopqrstuvwxyz
1234567890?!$%&
Agfa Corporation

CG Trump Mediaeval Bold Italic
ABCDEFGHIJKLMNOPQRSTUVWXYZ
abcdefghijklmnopqrstuvwxyz
1234567890?!$%&
Agfa Corporation

Univers™ 45 Light
ABCDEFGHIJKLMNOPQRSTUVWXYZ
abcdefghijklmnopqrstuvwxyz
1234567890?!$%&
Adobe Systems, Inc.

Univers 45 Light Oblique
ABCDEFGHIJKLMNOPQRSTUVWXYZ
abcdefghijklmnopqrstuvwxyz
1234567890?!$%&
Adobe Systems, Inc.

Univers 47 Condensed Light
ABCDEFGHIJKLMNOPQRSTUVWXYZ
abcdefghijklmnopqrstuvwxyz
1234567890?!$%&
Adobe Systems, Inc.

Univers 47 Condensed Light Oblique
ABCDEFGHIJKLMNOPQRSTUVWXYZ
abcdefghijklmnopqrstuvwxyz
1234567890?!$%&
Adobe Systems, Inc.

Univers 55
ABCDEFGHIJKLMNOPQRSTUVWXYZ
abcdefghijklmnopqrstuvwxyz
1234567890?!$%&
Adobe Systems, Inc.

Univers 55 Oblique
ABCDEFGHIJKLMNOPQRSTUVWXYZ
abcdefghijklmnopqrstuvwxyz
1234567890?!$%&
Adobe Systems, Inc.

Univers 57 Condensed
ABCDEFGHIJKLMNOPQRSTUVWXYZ
abcdefghijklmnopqrstuvwxyz
1234567890?!$%&
Adobe Systems, Inc.

Univers 57 Condensed Oblique
ABCDEFGHIJKLMNOPQRSTUVWXYZ
abcdefghijklmnopqrstuvwxyz
1234567890?!$%&
Adobe Systems, Inc.

Univers 65 Bold
ABCDEFGHIJKLMNOPQRSTUVWXYZ
abcdefghijklmnopqrstuvwxyz
1234567890?!$%&
Adobe Systems, Inc.

Univers 65 Bold Oblique
ABCDEFGHIJKLMNOPQRSTUVWXYZ
abcdefghijklmnopqrstuvwxyz
1234567890?!$%&
Adobe Systems, Inc.

Univers 67 Condensed Bold
ABCDEFGHIJKLMNOPQRSTUVWXYZ
abcdefghijklmnopqrstuvwxyz
1234567890?!$%&
Adobe Systems, Inc.

Univers 67 Condensed Bold Oblique
ABCDEFGHIJKLMNOPQRSTUVWXYZ
abcdefghijklmnopqrstuvwxyz
1234567890?!$%&
Adobe Systems, Inc.

Univers 75 Black
ABCDEFGHIJKLMNOPQRSTUVWXYZ
abcdefghijklmnopqrstuvwxyz
1234567890?!$%&
Adobe Systems, Inc.

Univers 75 Black Oblique
ABCDEFGHIJKLMNOPQRSTUVWXYZ
abcdefghijklmnopqrstuvwxyz
1234567890?!$%&
Adobe Systems, Inc.

University Roman
ABCDEFGHIJKLMNOPQRSTUVWXYZ
abcdefghijklmnopqrstuvwxyz
1234567890?!$%&
Adobe Systems, Inc.

Upstart

ABCDEFGHIJKLMNOPQRSTUVWXYZ

abcdefghijklmnopqrstuvwxyz

1234567890?!$%&

EmDash

Upstart Condensed

ABCDEFGHIJKLMNOPQRSTUVWXYZ

abcdefghijklmnopqrstuvwxyz

1234567890?!$%&

EmDash

Upstart Extended

ABCDEFGHIJKLMNOPQRSTUVWXYZ

abcdefghijklmnopqrstuvwxyz

1234567890?!$%&

EmDash

Utopia™

ABCDEFGHIJKLMNOPQRSTUVWXYZ

abcdefghijklmnopqrstuvwxyz

1234567890?!$%&

Adobe Systems, Inc.

Utopia Italic

ABCDEFGHIJKLMNOPQRSTUVWXYZ

abcdefghijklmnopqrstuvwxyz

1234567890?!$%&

Adobe Systems, Inc.

Utopia Bold

ABCDEFGHIJKLMNOPQRSTUVWXYZ
abcdefghijklmnopqrstuvwxyz
1234567890?!$%&

Adobe Systems, Inc.

Utopia Black

ABCDEFGHIJKLMNOPQRSTUVWXYZ
abcdefghijklmnopqrstuvwxyz
1234567890?!$%&

Adobe Systems, Inc.

Utopia Semibold

ABCDEFGHIJKLMNOPQRSTUVWXYZ
abcdefghijklmnopqrstuvwxyz
1234567890?!$%&

Adobe Systems, Inc.

Utopia Bold Italic

ABCDEFGHIJKLMNOPQRSTUVWXYZ
abcdefghijklmnopqrstuvwxyz
1234567890?!$%&

Adobe Systems, Inc.

Utopia Semibold Italic

ABCDEFGHIJKLMNOPQRSTUVWXYZ
abcdefghijklmnopqrstuvwxyz
1234567890?!$%&

Adobe Systems, Inc.

VAG Rounded Bold

ABCDEFGHIJKLMNOPQRSTUVWXYZ
abcdefghijklmnopqrstuvwxyz
1234567890?!$%&

Adobe Systems, Inc.

VAG Rounded Black

ABCDEFGHIJKLMNOPQRSTUVWXYZ
abcdefghijklmnopqrstuvwxyz
1234567890?!$%&

Adobe Systems, Inc.

VAG Rounded Light

ABCDEFGHIJKLMNOPQRSTUVWXYZ
abcdefghijklmnopqrstuvwxyz
1234567890?!$%&

Adobe Systems, Inc.

VAG Rounded Thin

ABCDEFGHIJKLMNOPQRSTUVWXYZ
abcdefghijklmnopqrstuvwxyz
1234567890?!$%&

Adobe Systems, Inc.

Versailles

ABCDEFGHIJKLMNOPQRSTUVWXYZ
abcdefghijklmnopqrstuvwxyz
1234567890?!$%&

Dubl-Click Software, Inc.

Versailles Bold
ABCDEFGHIJKLMNOPQRSTUVWXYZ
abcdefghijklmnopqrstuvwxyz
1234567890?!$%&

Dubl-Click Software, Inc.

Versailles Sans
ABCDEFGHIJKLMNOPQRSTUVWXYZ
abcdefghijklmnopqrstuvwxyz
1234567890?!$%&

Dubl-Click Software, Inc.

Versailles Sans Bold
ABCDEFGHIJKLMNOPQRSTUVWXYZ
abcdefghijklmnopqrstuvwxyz
1234567890?!$%&

Dubl-Click Software, Inc.

Walbaum®
ABCDEFGHIJKLMNOPQRSTUVWXYZ
abcdefghijklmnopqrstuvwxyz
1234567890?!$%&

Adobe Systems, Inc.

Walbaum Italic
ABCDEFGHIJKLMNOPQRSTUVWXYZ
abcdefghijklmnopqrstuvwxyz
1234567890?!$%&

Adobe Systems, Inc.

Walbaum Bold

ABCDEFGHIJKLMNOPQRSTUVWXYZ
abcdefghijklmnopqrstuvwxyz
1234567890?!$%&

Adobe Systems, Inc.

Walbaum Bold Italic

ABCDEFGHIJKLMNOPQRSTUVWXYZ
abcdefghijklmnopqrstuvwxyz
1234567890?!$%&

Adobe Systems, Inc.

Weiss®

ABCDEFGHIJKLMNOPQRSTUVWXYZ
abcdefghijklmnopqrstuvwxyz
1234567890?!$%&

Adobe Systems, Inc.

Weiss Italic

ABCDEFGHIJKLMNOPQRSTUVWXYZ
abcdefghijklmnopqrstuvwxyz
1234567890?!$%&

Adobe Systems, Inc.

Weiss Bold

ABCDEFGHIJKLMNOPQRSTUVWXYZ
abcdefghijklmnopqrstuvwxyz
1234567890?!$%&

Adobe Systems, Inc.

Weiss Extra Bold
ABCDEFGHIJKLMNOPQRSTUVWXYZ
abcdefghijklmnopqrstuvwxyz
1234567890?!$%&
Adobe Systems, Inc.

ITC Zapf Chancery®
ABCDEFGHIJKLMNOPQRSTUVWXYZ
abcdefghijklmnopqrstuvwxyz
1234567890?!$%&
Adobe Systems, Inc

4 Font Companies

This chapter shows you the complete line of English language, PostScript font packages from[1]

> Adobe® Systems, Inc.
> Agfa Corporation
> Alphabets, Inc.
> Devonian International Software Company
> Dubl-Click Software, Inc.
> EmDash™
> Studio 231
> T/Maker Company

In addition to font samples, you'll find each company's address and phone numbers as well as

- A brief company profile.

- A description of the product line.

- A legend that lets you know whether the fonts are only available for the Mac, or are also available for the IBM.

A list of foreign language and symbol fonts is found in the *Appendix*. For an alphabetical listing of fonts by font name, see Chapter 3, *Postscript Fonts*.

---

[1] Font companies are continually adding to their collections. Contact the companies directly for a list of their newest fonts.

Adobe

Adobe® Systems, Inc.
1585 Charleston Road
P.O. Box 7900
Mountain View, CA 94039
(800) 83-FONTS
(415) 962-2100

Adobe UK Ltd.,
Minex House,
55a High St.,
Wimbledon,
London, SW19 5BA
081 944 1298 TEL
081 944 1314 FAX

Macintosh
IBM

PostScript

Adobe® Systems, Inc. is the owner and licensor of *PostScript*, the most popular and widely-used page-description language for desktop publishing.

Adobe markets the *Adobe Type Library*, an extensive collection of PostScript fonts that are available in both Mac and IBM formats. Many fonts in the Adobe Type Library are created exclusively for Adobe by Adobe's own designers. Other products from Adobe include the

- *Adobe FontFolio*, the entire Adobe Type Library on a hard disk. The *Adobe FontFolio* attaches to any PostScript printer that has a SCSI port.

- *Adobe Type Manager*, a product for the Macintosh that significantly improves the appearance of PostScript screen-fonts.

Mac System - Hardware Requirements

- Two 800K disk drives *or* one disk drive and a hard disk.
- PostScript printer or typesetter.

IBM Systems - Hardware Requirements

- 512K of memory.
- A hard disk.
- PostScript printer or typesetter.

Package # 1

Palatino™
Palatino Italic
Palatino Bold
Palatino Bold Italic

Package # 2

ITC Bookman® Light
ITC Bookman Light Italic
ITC Bookman Demi
ITC Bookman Demi Italic

Package # 3

ITC Zapf Chancery®

Package # 4

ITC Avant Garde Gothic® Book
ITC Avant Garde Book Gothic Oblique
ITC Avant Garde Gothic Demi
ITC Avant Garde Gothic Demi Oblique

Package # 5

New Century Schoolbook
New Century Schoolbook Italic
New Century Schoolbook Bold
New Century Schoolbook Bold Italic

Package # 6

Optima™
Optima Oblique
Optima Bold
Optima Bold Oblique

Package # 7

ITC Souvenir®
ITC Souvenir Light Italic
ITC Souvenir Demi
ITC Souvenir Demi Italic

Package # 8

ITC Lubalin Graph® Book
ITC Lubalin Graph Book Oblique
ITC Lubalin Graph Demi
ITC Lubalin Graph Demi Oblique

Package # 9

ITC Garamond® Light
ITC Garamond Light Italic
ITC Garamond Bold
ITC Garamond Bold Italic

Package # 10

ITC MACHINE®
ITC American Typewriter®
ITC American Typewriter Bold

Package # 11

ITC Benguiat®
ITC Benguiat Bold
ITC Friz Quadrata®
ITC Friz Quadrata Bold

Package # 12

Glypha™
Glypha Oblique
Glypha Bold
Glypha Bold Oblique

Package # 13

Helvetica™ Light
Helvetica Light Oblique
Helvetica Black
Helvetica Black Oblique

Package # 14

Helvetica Condensed Light
Helvetica Condensed Light Oblique
Helvetica Condensed
Helvetica Condensed Oblique
Helvetica Condensed Bold
Helvetica Condensed Bold Oblique
Helvetica Condensed Black
Helvetica Condensed Black Oblique

Package # 15

Trump Mediæval™
Trump Mediæval Italic
Trump Mediæval Bold
Trump Mediæval Bold Italic

Package # 16

Melior™
Melior Italic
Melior Bold
Melior Bold Italic

Package # 17

ITC Galliard® Roman
ITC Galliard Italic
ITC Galliard Bold
ITC Galliard Bold Italic

Package # 18

ITC New Baskerville® Roman
ITC New Baskerville Italic
ITC New Baskerville Bold
ITC New Baskerville Bold Italic

Package # 19

ITC Korinna® Regular
ITC Korinna Kursiv Regular
ITC Korinna Bold
ITC Korinna Kursiv Bold

Package # 20

Goudy Old Style
Goudy Old Style Italic
Goudy Old StyleBold
Goudy Old Style Bold Italic

Package # 22

Century Old Style
Century Old Style Italic
Century Old Style Bold

Package # 23

ITC Franklin Gothic® Book
ITC Franklin Gothic Book Oblique
ITC Franklin Gothic Demi
ITC Franklin Gothic Demi Oblique
ITC Franklin Gothic Heavy
ITC Franklin Gothic Heavy Oblique

Package # 24

ITC Cheltenham® Book
ITC Cheltenham Book Italic
ITC Cheltenham Bold
ITC Cheltenham Bold Italic

Package # 25

Park Avenue®

Package # 26

Bodoni
Bodoni Italic
Bodoni Bold
Bodoni Bold Italic
Bodoni Poster

Package # 27

Letter Gothic
Letter Gothic Slanted
Letter Gothic Bold
Letter Gothic Bold Slanted

Package # 28

Prestige Elite
Prestige Elite Slanted
Prestige Elite Bold
Prestige Elite Bold Slanted

Package # 29

ORATOR
ORATOR SLANTED

Package # 30

News Gothic
News Gothic Oblique
News Gothic Bold
News Gothic Bold Oblique

Package # 31

ITC Tiffany®
ITC Tiffany Italic
ITC Tiffany Demi
ITC Tiffany Demi Italic
ITC Tiffany Heavy
ITC Tiffany Heavy Italic

Package # 32

Cooper Black
Cooper Black Italic

Package # 33

STENCIL
Hobo
Brush Script

Package # 34

Aachen Bold
Revue
University Roman
Freestyle Script

Package # 36

Lucida® Roman
Lucida Italic
Lucida Bold
Lucida Bold Italic

Package # 37

Univers™ 45 Light
Univers 45 Light Oblique
Univers 55
Univers 55 Oblique
Univers 65 Bold
Univers 65 Bold Oblique
Univers 75 Black
Univers 75 Black Oblique

Package # 38

Univers 47 Condensed Light
Univers 47 Condensed Light Oblique
Univers 57 Condensed
Univers 57 Condensed Oblique
Univers 67 Condensed Bold
Univers 67 Condensed Bold Oblique

Package # 39

Futura® Light
Futura Light Oblique
Futura Book
Futura Book Oblique
Futura Bold
Futura Bold Oblique

Package # 40

Stone® Serif
Stone Serif Italic
Stone Serif Semibold
Stone Serif Semibold Italic
Stone Serif Bold
Stone Serif Bold Italic

Package # 41

Stone Sans
Stone Sans Italic
Stone Sans Semibold
Stone Sans Semibold Italic
Stone Sans Bold
Stone Sans Bold Italic

Package # 42

Stone Informal
Stone Informal Italic
Stone Informal Semibold
Stone Informal Semibold Italic
Stone Informal Bold
Stone Informal Bold Italic

Package # 43

Corona™
Corona Italic
Corona Bold

Package # 44

Eurostile®
Eurostile Oblique
Eurostile Demi
Eurostile Demi Oblique
Eurostile Bold
Eurostile Bold Oblique

Package # 45

Excelsior™
Excelsior Italic
Excelsior Bold

Package # 46

Futura
Futura Oblique
Futura Heavy
Futura Heavy Oblique
Futura Extra Bold
Futura Extra Bold Oblique

Package # 47

Futura Condensed Light
Futura Condensed Light Oblique
Futura Condensed
Futura Condensed Oblique
Futura Condensed Bold
Futura Condensed Bold Oblique
Futura Condensed Extra Bold
Futura Condensed Extra Bold Oblique

Package # 48

Lucida Sans Roman
Lucida Sans Italic
Lucida Sans Bold
Lucida Sans Bold Italic

Package # 49

Memphis™ Light
Memphis Light Italic
Memphis Medium
Memphis Medium Italic
Memphis Bold
Memphis Bold Italic
Memphis Extra Bold

Package # 50

Helvetica Compressed
Helvetica Compressed Extra
Helvetica Compressed Ultra

Package #51

Italia Book
Italia Medium
Italia Bold

Package # 52

Belwe Light
Belwe Medium
Belwe Bold
Belwe Condensed

Package # 53

Caslon 540 Roman
Caslon 540 Italic
Caslon 3 Roman
Caslon 3 Italic

Package # 54

Goudy Extra Bold
Goudy Heavyface
Goudy Heavyface Italic

Package # 55

Janson Text™
Janson Text Italic
Janson Text Bold
Janson Text Bold Italic

Package # 56

ITC Eras® Light
ITC Eras Book
ITC Eras Medium
ITC Eras Demi
ITC Eras Bold
ITC Eras Ultra

Package # 57

ITC Kabel® Book
ITC Kabel Medium
ITC Kabel Demi
ITC Kabel Bold
ITC Kabel Ultra

Package # 58

OCRA
OCRB

Package # 59

Helvetica 25 Ultra Light
Helvetica 26 Ultra Light Italic
Helvetica 95 Black
Helvetica 96 Black Italic

Package # 60

Helvetica 35 Thin
Helvetica 36 Thin Italic
Helvetica 55 Roman
Helvetica 56 Italic
Helvetica 75 Bold
Helvetica 76 Bold Italic

Package # 61

Helvetica 45 Light
Helvetica 46 Light Italic
Helvetica 65 Medium
Helvetica 66 Medium Italic
Helvetica 85 Heavy
Helvetica 86 Heavy Italic

Package # 62

Times™ Ten Roman
Times Ten Italic
Times Ten Bold
Times Ten Bold Italic

Package # 63

Kaufmann®
Kaufmann Bold

Package # 64

Clarendon™ Light
Clarendon
Clarendon Bold

Package # 65

Peignot™ Light
Peignot Demi
Peignot Bold

Package # 66

New Caledonia™
New Caledonia Italic
New Caledonia Semi Bold
New Caledonia Semi Bold Italic
New Caledonia Bold
New Caledonia Bold Italic
New Caledonia Black
New Caledonia Black Italic

Package # 67

ITC Clearface® Regular
ITC Clearface Regular Italic
ITC Clearface Bold
ITC Clearface Bold Italic
ITC Clearface Heavy
ITC Clearface Heavy Italic
ITC Clearface Black
ITC Clearface Black Italic

Package # 68

Americana®
Americana Italic
Americana Bold
Americana Extra Bold

Package # 69

ITC Serif Gothic® Light
ITC Serif Gothic
ITC Serif Gothic Bold
ITC Serif Gothic Extra Bold
ITC Serif Gothic Heavy
ITC Serif Gothic Black

Package # 70

Century Expanded
Century Expanded Italic

Package # 71

Serifa® 45 Light
Serifa 46 Light Italic
Serifa 55
Serifa 56 Italic
Serifa 65 Bold
Serifa 75 Black

Package # 72

Caslon Open Face

Package # 73

Frutiger™ 45 Light
Frutiger 46 Light Italic
Frutiger 55
Frutiger 56 Italic
Frutiger 65 Bold
Frutiger 66 Bold Italic
Frutiger 75 Black
Frutiger 76 Black Italic
Frutiger 95 Ultra Black

Package # 74

Linotype Centennial™ 45 Light
Linotype Centennial 46 Light Italic
Linotype Centennial 55
Linotype Centennial 56 Italic
Linotype Centennial 75 Bold
Linotype Centennial 76 Bold Italic
Linotype Centennial 95 Black
Linotype Centennial 96 Black Italic

Package # 75

Stemple Garamond™ Roman
Stemple Garamond Italic
Stemple Garamond Bold
Stemple Garamond Bold Italic

Package # 76

Weiss®
Weiss Italic
Weiss Bold
Weiss Extra Bold

Package # 77

Garamond 3™
Garamond 3 Italic
Garamond 3 Bold
Garamond 3 Bold Italic

Package # 79

Avenir™ 35 Light
Avenir 35 Light Oblique
Avenir 55 Roman
Avenir 55 Oblique
Avenir 85 Heavy
Avenir 85 Heavy Oblique

Package # 80

Avenir 45 Book
Avenir 45 Book Oblique
Avenir 65 Medium
Avenir 65 Medium Oblique
Avenir 95 Black
Avenir 95 Black Oblique

Package # 81

Walbaum®
Walbaum Italic
Walbaum Bold
Walbaum Bold Italic

Package # 82

Antique Olive™ Light
Antique Olive
Antique Olive Italic
Antique Olive Bold
Antique Olive Black

Package # 83

Life® Roman
Life Italic
Life Bold

Package # 84

Concorde®
Concorde Italic
Concorde Bold
Concorde Bold Italic

Package # 85

Gothic 13
Tempo™ Heavy Condensed
Tempo Heavy Condensed Italic

Package # 86

Cochin™
Cochin Italic
Cochin Bold
Cochin Bold Italic

Package # 87

ITC Bauhaus™ Light
ITC Bauhaus Medium
ITC Bauhaus Demi
ITC Bauhaus Bold
ITC Bauhaus Heavy

Package #88

Sabon™ Roman
Sabon Italic
Sabon Bold
Sabon Bold Italic

Package # 89

Hiroshige™ Book
Hiroshige Book Italic
Hiroshige Medium
Hiroshige Medium Italic
Hiroshige Bold
Hiroshige Bold Italic
Hiroshige Black
Hiroshige Black Italic

Package # 90

Arnold Böcklin
Fette Fraktur
Helvetica Inserat
Present™ Script

Package # 91

Dom Casual
Dom Casual Bold

Package # 92

Post Antiqua™
Post Antiqua Bold

Package # 93

Folio® Light
Folio Medium
Folio Bold
Folio Extra Bold
Folio Bold Condensed

Package # 94

Linoscript™
Linotext™

Package # 95

VAG Rounded Thin
VAG Rounded Light
VAG Rounded Bold
VAG Rounded Black

Package # 96

Akzidenz Grotesk® Light
Akzidenz Grotesk Roman
Akzidenz Grotesk Bold
Akzidenz Grotesk Black

Package # 97

Impressum® Roman
Impressum Italic
Impressum Bold

Package # 98

Bauer Bodoni® Roman
Bauer Bodoni Italic
Bauer Bodoni Bold
Bauer Bodoni Bold Italic

Package # 99

New Aster®
New Aster Italic
New Aster Semi Bold
New Aster Semi Bold Italic
New Aster Bold
New Aster Bold Italic
New Aster Black
New Aster Black Italic

Package # 100

Adobe Garamond™ Regular
Adobe Garamond Italic
Adobe Garamond Semibold
Adobe Garamond Semibold Italic
Adobe Garamond Bold
Adobe Garamond Bold Italic

Package # 101

ADOBE GARAMOND EXPERT COLLECTION
TITLING CAPITALS
ALTERNATE ITALIC

Package # 102

Cándida® Roman
Cándida Italic
Cándida Bold

Package # 103

Franklin Gothic Extra Condensed
Franklin Gothic Condensed
Franklin Gothic No. 2 Roman

Package # 104

Utopia™
Utopia Italic
Utopia Semibold
Utopia Semibold Italic
Utopia Bold
Utopia Bold Italic
Utopia Black

AGFA

AGFA Compugraphic Division
90 Industrial Way
Wilmington, MA 01887
(800) 622-TYPE Sales
(508) 658-5600 Information
(508) 657-5328 FAX

Agfa UK Ltd.,
Sandbeck Way,
Wetherby,
W. Yorkshire
LS22 4DN
0937 61944 TEL
0937 61174 FAX

Macintosh
IBM

PostScript

AGFA Corporation is the parent company of *AGFA Compugraphic Division*, a font technology unit which develops and markets fonts. AGFA Compugraphic licenses many of their typefaces--some bearing the famous *CG* logo--to other font companies. Three separate type libraries make up the *Agfa Type Collection*.

- The *Studio™ Series* is a collection of PostScript typefaces developed exclusively for the Macintosh. The Studio Series was previously known as *CG Type*. Samples from this type library begin on the following page.

- The *Professional™ Series* is the complete *Adobe Type Library*. The Professional Series complements the Studio Series by offering an extensive collection of PostScript fonts in both Mac and IBM formats. Samples from the *Adobe Type Library* begin on page 169.

- *Type Director™* fonts. Type Director is a typeface scaling and font-management software for IBM computers. It was co-developed by AGFA Compugraphic and Hewlett Packard.

Mac System - Hardware Requirements

- System Software 6.0 (or later).
- Two 800K disk drives *or* one disk drive and a hard disk.
- PostScript printer or typesetter.

IBM Systems - Hardware Requirements

Professional Series

- 512K of memory.
- A hard disk.
- PostScript printer or typesetter.

Volume # 1

Garth Graphic®
Garth Graphic Italic
Garth Graphic Bold
Garth Graphic Bold Italic

Volume # 2

Antique Olive
Antique Olive Italic
Antique Olive Medium
Antique Olive Medium Italic

Volume # 3

CG Collage
CG Collage Italic
CG Collage Bold
CG Collage Bold Italic

Volume # 4

CGTrump Mediaeval
CGTrump Mediaeval Italic
CGTrump Mediaeval Bold
CGTrump Mediaeval Bold Italic

Volume # 5

Garamond Antiqua
Garamond Kursiv
Garamond Halbfett
Garamond Kursiv Halbfett

Volume # 6

CG Nashville Medium
CG Nashville Medium Italic
CG Nashville Bold
CG Nashville Bold Italic

Volume # 7

ITC Novarese® Book
ITC Novarese Book Italic
ITC Novarese Bold
ITC Novarese Bold Italic

Volume # 8

Schneidler
Schneidler Italic
Schneidler Bold
Schneidler Bold Italic

Volume # 9

Shannon Book™
Shannon Oblique
Shannon Bold
Shannon Extrabold

Volume # 10

CG Symphony
CG Symphony Italic
CG Symphony Bold
CG Symphony Black

191

Volume # 11

CG Triumvirate™
CG Triumvirate Italic
CG Triumvirate Bold
CG Triumvirate Bold Italic

Volume # 12

Goudy Heavyface
Goudy Heavyface Italic
Goudy Heavyface Condensed

Volume # 13

Branding Iron
Isabella
McCullough
Raphael

Volume # 14

CG Frontiera 55
CG Frontiera 56
CG Frontiera 65
CG Frontiera 66

Volume # 15

CG Triumvirate Inserat
CG Triumvirate Inserat Italic
CG Triumvirate Inserat Compressed
CG Triumvirate Inserat Extra Compressed

Volume # 16

Raleigh Light
Raleigh Medium
Raleigh Bold
Raleigh Extrabold

Volume # 17

Aquarius No. 8
Clarendon Book Condensed
CG Poster Bodoni
CG Poster Bodoni Italic

Volume # 18

ITC Bauhaus® Light
ITC Bauhaus Medium
ITC Bauhaus Bold
ITC Bauhaus Heavy

Volume # 19

ITC Clearface® Regular
ITC Clearface Regular Italic
ITC Clearface Bold
ITC Clearface Bold Italic

Volume # 20

ITC Berkeley® Oldstyle Book
ITC Berkeley Oldstyle Book Italic
ITC Berkeley Oldstyle Bold
ITC Berkeley OldstyleBold Italic

Volume # 21

ITC Fenice® Regular
ITC Fenice Regular Italic
ITC Fenice Bold
ITC Fenice Bold Italic

193

Volume # 22

> VGC Egyptian 505 Light
> **VGC Egyptian 505**
> **VGC Egyptian 505 Medium**
> **VGC Egyptian 505 Bold**

Volume # 23

> **Antique Olive Bold**
> **Antique Olive Nord**
> ***Antique Olive Nord Italic***
> **Antique Olive Compact**

Volume # 24

> Impressum
> *Impressum Italic*
> **Impressum Bold**
> ***Impressum Bold Italic***

Volume # 25

> Méridien™ Light
> *Méridien Light Italic*
> **Méridien Bold**
> **Méridien Black**

Volume # 26

> Globe Gothic Light
> Globe Gothic Demi
> **Globe Gothic Bold**
> **Globe Gothic Ultra**

Alphabets

Alphabets, Inc.
P.O. Box 5448
Evanston, IL 60204
(800) 326-4086   Sales
(708) 328-2733   Information
(708) 657-5328   FAX

FontWorks UK Ltd   Macintosh
65-69 East Rd,
London N1 6AH   PostScript
071 490 5390 TEL
071 490 5391 FAX

Letters are one of the most pervasive signs of human culture, behind perhaps, only architecture in their omnipresence, says Peter Fraterdeus, president and design director of **Alphabets, Inc.**

Alphabets, Inc. offers a limited but high-quality collection of PostScript fonts for the Macintosh. Upon request, samples are available for most products.

Alphabets publishes a journal called *MiceType*™ which covers Letterform Design, Microcomputer Typography, and Macintosh Design Applications.

In 1989, Alphabets formed the *Alphabets Design Group* which offers

- PostScript conversion services.

- Custom design of alphabets and type.

- Graphic-arts system integration.

- Multi-media services for interactive presentations and software demos.

Mac System - Hardware Requirements

- No special requirements.

Prospera Disk™

Prospera

Prospera Italic

Egyptian Disk

Egyptian Bold Condensed

Small Egyptian Bold Condensed

DISC

Devonian International Software Company	Kuma Computers Ltd., 12 Horseshoe Park, Pangbourne, Berks RG8 7JW	Macintosh
P.O. Box 2351 Montclair, CA 91763 (714) 621-0973	0734 844335 TEL 0734 844339 FAX	PostScript

Devonian International Software Company was founded in 1985 by Dr. Elliot Weinstein--a practicing pediatrician--and Mr. Glenn Mitchell, a manufacturing engineer in the aerospace industry. DISC designs fonts and clip-art. They also offer a service that converts company logos to a font. (Samples from DISC's clip-art package are shown in Chapter 6, *Graphic Companies*.)

DISC offers a small collection of English-language fonts for Postscript laser printers (see the following page). Much more extensive,however, is their unique collection of display and foreign language fonts for dot matrix printers.

DISC's offering of foreign language fonts is eclectic and features such selections as Angerthas (runes), Gaelic, and Egyptian Hieroglyphs. DISC says that many of their products are the direct result of phone calls and letters from customers. (A complete list of foreign language fonts may be found in the *Appendix*.)

Devonia itself is a fictional country named after Devonshire, England. The *Devonian International Cookbook* is available from DISC and features recipes, folklore, and history about Devonia.

Mac System - Hardware Requirements

- PostScript printer or typesetter.

LASERgenix™
Newport News

Newport News

LASERgenix™
Fontana

Fontana

LASERgenix™
Riverside

Riverside

Riverside Italic

Riverside Bold

Dubl-Click

Dubl-Click Software, Inc.	Kuma Computers Ltd.,	
9316 Deering Avenue	12 Horseshoe Park,	Macintosh
Chatsworth, CA 91311	Pangbourne,	
(818) 700-9525	Berks RG8 7JW	PostScript
	0734 844335 TEL	
	0734 844339 FAX	

Dubl-Click Software, Inc. was founded in 1985 by Cliff Joyce, a graphic designer, and an assembly language programmer named Austin Durbin. The company's PostScript font line is called *World Class LaserType* and includes several font collections designed specifically for PostScript printers (see the following pages). Dubl-Click's other products and services include

- *Logos On Line*, a service that converts a logo to a PostScript font.

- *World Class Fonts*, a variety of bit-mapped fonts for dot matrix printers.

- *Wet Paint*, a series of graphics packages in the MacPaint format. (Samples are included in the *Dubl-Click* section of Chapter 6, *Graphics Companies*.)

- *Pattern Mover* and *Art Roundup*, two desk accessories included with Wet Paint products.

Mac System - Hardware Requirements

- One 800K disk drives.
- PostScript printer or typesetter.

Disk # 1

Aukland

CALAIS

CALAIS BOLD

Metropolitan

Disk # 2

Hoboken

IXTAPA BOLD

Saigon

Disk # 3

VERSAILLES

VERSAILLES Bold

VERSAILLES Sans

VERSAILLES Sans Bold

Disk # 5

Hancock Park Light

Hancock Park

Hancock Park Bold

Disk # 7

Frankfurt

Frankfurt Medium

Frankfurt Bold

Frankfurt Ultra

Disk # 8

Santa Monica
Santa Monica Bold
Santa Monica Ultra

Disk # 9

Aspen
Aspen Bold
Aspen Ultra

EmDash

EmDash
P.O. Box 8526
Northfield, IL   60093
(312) 441-6699

FontWorks UK Ltd
65-69 East Rd,
London N1 6AH
071 490 5390 TEL
071 490 5391 FAX

Macintosh

PostScript

EmDash offers two font collections for Postscript Printers (see the following page).

FONTSET 1 includes fourteen English-language fonts and four symbol fonts.   (For a listing of symbol fonts, please see the *Appendix*.)

FONTSET 2 includes eight English-language fonts and ten fraction fonts.   The fraction fonts add or substitute fraction characters for some of the math and diacritical characters that are already resident in your PostScript laser printer. There are separate fonts for

- Avant Garde
- Courier
- Helvetica
- Times Roman

NOTE: One or more of the fonts listed above must be resident in your PostScript laser printer in order for the fraction fonts to work on your system.

Mac System – Hardware Requirements

- System Software 6.0 (or later).
- *Font/DA Mover* 3.8 (or later).
- One 800K disk drive.
- PostScript printer or typesetter.

Volume # 1

ArchiText®
ArchiText Condensed
ArchiText Bold
ArchiText Bold Condensed
Briar™ Book
Briar Bold
Briar Heavy
Caspian™ Book
Caspian Condensed
Caspian Bold
Caspian Bold Condensed
UpStart™
UpStart Condensed
UpStart Extended

Volume # 2

GENDARME™ HEAVY
PALOMAR™ Bold
Konway™ Book
Konway Book Condensed
Konway Bold
Konway Bold Condensed
Konway Heavy
Konway Heavy Condensed

Studio 231

Studio 231
231 Bedford Avenue
Bellmore, NY 11710
(516) 785-4422
(516) 785-4173   FAX

Type Technologies Ltd.,   Macintosh
Euston House,
81-103 Euston St.,
London NW1 2ET   PostScript
071 387 5666 TEL
071 753 0234 FAX

Studio 231 is a full-service art studio that has released several English-language and symbol fonts for PostScript printers. (For a complete list of symbol fonts, see the *Appendix*.)   Studio 231 offers several graphic-related services including

- Art work and mechanical.

- Conventional typesetting.

- Output services (printing your original on a typesetter).

- Pantone color matching for transfers and line art.

Studio 231 also distributes *Kern-Rite*, a program which lets you customize the kerning of letter pairs. Kern-Rite is compatible with all PostScript fonts for the Macintosh. Kerned pairs will print correctly with most programs that support kerning.

NOTE: Many of Studio 231's type styles are best suited for display. As a result, some of them do not reproduce well in 14pt--the size of the samples--when printed at 300 dpi.[1] Much better results can be achieved with a typesetter.

Mac System - Hardware Requirements

- PostScript printer or typesetter.

---

[1] Three fonts were excluded from the samples due to their poor reproduction quality. Two were excluded from Volume #7; one was excluded from Volume #14.

Volume # 1

SBroadway
SBroadway Engraved
SCALLIA
SFolkwang
SSINGLE PIPE
SDOUBLE PIPE

Volume # 2

SBradley Outline
S Basilea
SRevue
SRICCARDO
SRound Black
SBolt Bold

Volume # 3

SBradley
SBANCO
SBlock
SBALLON EXTRA BOLD
SBRUCE MIKITA
SBrody Display

Volume # 4

SBaker Argentina No. 1
SBaker Argentina No. 1 Italic
SBaker Argentina No. 2
SBaker Argentina No. 2 Italic
SBaker Argentina No. 3
SBaker Argentina No. 3 Italic

Volume # 5

SBaker Argentina No. 4
SBaker Argentina No. 4 Italic
SBaker Argentina No. 5
SBaker Argentina No. 5 Italic
SBaker Argentina No. 6
SBaker Argentina No. 6 Italic

Volume # 6

SBaker Danmark One
SBaker Danmark Two
SBaker Danmark Three
SDUO SOLID
SCORNBALL
SCARTOON BOLD

Volume # 7

SBurgondy Right
SBritannic
SFutura Black
SBURGESE BLACK

Volume # 9

SLED 16
SMOORE COMPUTER
SAdlibs
SAnzeigen Grotesk Bold
SBarry Medium
SBarry Bold

Volume # 10

SGill Sans Light
SGill Sans Light Italic
SGill Sans
SGill Sans Italic
SGill Sans Bold
SGill Sans Bold Italic

Volume # 11

SAlbertus
SAlbertusInline
SAlbertus Outline
SALBERTUS TITLING
SALBERTUS BOLD TITLING
SALBERTUS BLACK

Volume # 12

SStandard Light
SStandard
SStandard Medium
SStandard Bold
SStandard Condensed
SStandard Medium Condensed

Volume # 13

SStandard Bold Condensed
SStandard Extra Bold Condensed
SStandard Extra Light Extended
SStandard Light Extended
SStandard Extended
SStd. Extra Bold Extended

207

Volume # 14

SThreshold
SStark Debonair
SStark Debonair Semi Bold
SStark Debonair Mono Bold
SSTEELPLATE GOTHIC BOLD

Volume # 15

SSerpentine Light
SSerpentine Medium
SSerpentine Bold
SSerpentine Bold Italic
SSThorowgood Roman
SSThorowgood Italic

Volume # 16

SACCANT
STHUNDERBIRD EXTRA CONDENSED
SGill Sans Extra Bold Condensed
SGill Sans Bold Condensed
SGill Sans Extra Bold
SGill Sans Ultra Bold

Volume # 17

SSyntax
SSyntax Bold
SSyntax Ultra Bold
STango
ST.H.ALPHABET SOUP
SFrozen Alaska

Volume # 18

SRussell Square

SRussell Square Italic

SRussell Square Light

SRussell Square Light Italic

SRussell Square Extra Light

SRussell Square Extra Light Italic

Volume # 19

SFreehand

SRussell Square Bold

SRussell Square Extra Bold

SAbbott Oldstyle

SAndromeda

SAndromeda Extra Bold

Volume # 20

SAngular

SAngular Black

SAngular Black Extended

SAngular Open

SBeads

SBulletin Typewriter

Volume # 21

SCloister Open Face

SCactus Light

SCactus Bold

SCactus Extra Bold

SCactus Black

SCHINA

T/Maker

T/Maker Company
1390 Villa Street
Mountain View, CA   94041
(415) 962-0195
(415) 962-0201   FAX

Persona,   Unit 1,
Silver Glade Bus. Park,   Macintosh
Leatherhead Rd,
Chessington,   PostScript
Surrey KT9 2NQ
03727 29611 TEL
03727 43535 FAX

T/Maker Company was founded in 1979. Their product line includes three PostScript font packages for the Macintosh and several graphic packages for both the Mac and the IBM. (More information on T/Maker as well as samples from their graphic packages can be found in the T/Maker section of Chapter 6, *Graphic Companies*.)

T/Maker's PostScript font packages are called *LaserLetters* (see the following page). Each package includes one type style and a complete range of foreign language characters.

T/Maker's also offers two bit-mapped letter packages for dot matrix printers: *Letters 1* and *Letters 2*. These collections may be used with any MacPaint-compatible program and then inserted into your page layout using the scrapbook or clipboard. Several large sizes from 24-72pt. are included.

Mac System - Hardware Requirements

* PostScript printer or typesetter.

210

Bombay • LaserLetters

Bombay
Bombay Gray

Plymouth • LaserLetters

Plymouth
Plymouth Gray

Seville • LaserLetters

Seville
Seville Gray

5 Working With Graphics

Images give visual impact to your documents and presentation materials. From computers, to business, to retail, to medical, to sports, to travel, to fitness, to real estate--there are tens of thousands of images to choose from.

Many companies offer collections of clip-art for specific applications or industries (e.g., borders, computers, and business images). Other companies include a potpourri of clip-art that can be used in a variety of situations. See Chapter 6, *Clip-Art Companies*, for samples from over ninety products.

This chapter discusses clip-art basics such as scaling images correctly, working with different graphic formats, and staying within the copyright law.

Clip-Art Basics

What's In A Name?

Clip-Art, Graphics, Images, Electronic Art--these words all refer to electronically-stored pictures, yet each company uses different words to describe the same technology.

It's confusing enough with companies using different words to describe electronic images. To complicate matters, many words that are used to describe electronic images have

212

a different meaning to artists and printers.

For example, *graphics* is often used to describe hand-drawn illustrations; *images* also refers to photographs; and *clip-art* has a meaning all its own.

Clip-art gets its name from art images that are sold on large, printed sheets. The art is clipped-out from the page with a scissors and then pasted (with glue) onto a page layout. This type of clip-art is still used today and is offered by some of the same companies that offer *electronic art*.

What Do You Get?

Most clip-art packages, at minimum, come with a booklet that

- Shows you all of the images in the collection.

- Tells you the name of each image-file on the diskette(s).

Some companies also include an index of the images and/or a booklet of suggestions for using the graphics effectively.

Subscription Services

Subscription services are another name for clip-art clubs. You pay the company a monthly or quarterly fee and they send you new releases of clip-art on a regular basis.

Copyright

When you purchase a clip-art package, you do not become the owner of the artwork. Whether or not a copyright notice appears next to each image, all the images are either copyrighted individually or as part of the collection.

Your rights to use the clip-art are spelled out in the manufacturer's *License Agreement*. Read the agreement very carefully--it explains how the *owner* of the clip-art (the manufacturer) is letting the *licensee* (you) use the images. Understanding your license now can help you and your company avoid legal trouble later on.

The license will not allow you to make copies of the clip-art to give away or sell, nor will it give you the right to include the clip-art in other collections you intend to sell. It may also place limitations on your use of the art in advertisements.

What you're typically *allowed* to do is make one backup copy of the original diskette(s) and use the art in your own documents without restriction.

Scaling Clip-Art

Many paint, draw, and page layout programs let you resize (*scale*) your clip-art. Keeping your art in correct proportion while scaling can be a little tricky.

For example, enlarging a 2x3-inch image by one inch in both height and width will not keep the image in proportion since 1-inch is a 50% increase to the 2-inch side but only a 33% increase to the 3-inch side. To correctly scale a 2x3-inch image 50% larger, you need to add 1-inch to the 2-inch side and 1.5-inches to the 3-inch side. (Samples of scaling are shown on the following page.)

Paint and Draw Programs

Traditionally, paint programs and draw programs each created a specific type of graphic with advantages and disadvantages.

214

Scaling Clip-Art

These illustrations were created using *Graphics Composer* from Arts & Letters.

Today, graphic manipulation programs combine paint-style features with draw-style features in an attempt to offer the best of both worlds.

Paint Programs

Paint programs were the first graphic-manipulation programs available for the Macintosh. Images created with these programs are called paint or *bit-mapped* graphics because the screen is painted by turning individual *bits* (screen-pixels) on and off.

Paint programs provide tools for drawing and erasing basic shapes (e.g., lines, circles, and squares). Many also offer a feature that magnifies a small portion of the screen so that each pixel may be manipulated individually.

Bit-mapped graphics print more quickly (except when stored in the TIFF format) and display shades of gray better than graphics that are created with draw programs.

Disadvantages of bit-mapped graphics are that the graphics cannot easily be rotated or colored, and tend to lose detail when scaled.

Draw Programs

Draw programs create images by describing their size, shape, and position on the screen. They rely on a special program in the Mac called *Quick Draw*. Quick Draw interprets the movements you make with the mouse and tells the screen how to display the objects.

Graphics created with draw programs are called object-oriented graphics because the images are created using a series of objects (e.g., rectangles, ovals, and polygons) rather than individual pixels. Object-oriented graphics exist as a whole and can only be manipulated as a whole.

An advantage to object-oriented graphics is that they can be scaled and rotated without distortion. A limitation of draw programs is that they cannot handle irregularly-shaped objects, such as those that are drawn free-hand.

Graphic File Formats

Whether you create an image using a graphic manipulation program or work with a commercial clip-art image, the graphic file is likely to be stored in one of three formats.

- PICT
- TIFF
- EPS

PICT Files

PICT is bit-mapped file format. The resolution (dpi) of the image is determined by the program that saves the file. PICT is the file format used by most paint programs although some draw-style programs can also save a file in this format. (Once a draw-style program has saved an image as a bit-map, it can then be edited by a paint program.)

TIFF Files

The *TIFF* format is used for scanned images. TIFF is an acronym for *Tagged Image File Format*. TIFF files contain a bit-mapped image for the screen display and a separate set of instructions that describe how the image should be printed.

217

One problem with TIFF is that it does not have a standard format. Many companies use their own set of TIFF instructions for the three types of TIFF files.

- Bi-level TIFF.

- Halftone TIFF.

- Gray-scale TIFF.

Bi-level TIFF

This TIFF format is generally used when scanned images contain few or no gray tones. *Bi-level TIFF* file-formats are small and easy to manage.

Halftone TIFF

Halftone or *dithered TIFF* has patterns of black and white dots that represent the gray tones. Scaling halftone TIFF images can result in a *moire* pattern, a checkerboard effect that occurs when the printer cannot accommodate the number of dots-per-inch of the image.

Gray-scale TIFF

This file format is used when an image contains many shades of gray.

EPS Files

EPS is an acronym for *Encapsulated PostScript*. EPS graphics are object-oriented graphics written in the PostScript language. The PostScript file includes English-language instructions that you can actually *read* on your screen.

EPS files always include instructions that can be interpreted by a PostScript printer for printing the graphic. The file usually (but not always) includes a screen image that allows you to view the image on your monitor.

6 Graphic Companies

This chapter is your source for clip-art for the Macintosh. On these pages you'll find several hundred clip-art samples from over ninety different graphic packages.

Where space permits, we show you an average of 10% of the images in each clip-art package. Each collection was reviewed in its entirety. The samples on the following pages are representative of the entire clip-art collection.

We counted the graphics in each package and have displayed that number on the first page of each layout for each collection (just under the name of the collection).

Some clip-art collections received two pages in the *Red Book* while others received only one. The determining factor was the number of graphics in the package. When a package includes at least 135 separate images, the collection received two pages. When the package includes less than 135 separate images, it received one page in the *Red Book*.

In this chapter you'll find clip-art from

> 3G Graphics
> Archive Arts
> Devonian International Software Company
> Dream Maker Software™
> Dubl-Click Software, Inc.
> Dynamic Graphics, Inc.
> Eykon Computer Graphics
> MGI (Marketing Graphics, Inc.)
> Metro ImageBase™, Inc.
> Multi-Ad Services, Inc.™

One Mile Up, Inc.
Qualitas Trading Company
Silicon Designs
Studio Advertising Art
T/Maker Company

In addition to clip-art samples, you'll find

- Each company's address and phone numbers.

- A brief company profile.

- A description of the product line.

- A legend that lets you know whether the graphics are only available for the Mac, or are also available for the IBM.

- A legend that lists the graphic formats available and the printer output (dpi) for each format.

3G

3G Graphics
11410 N.E. 124th Street
Suite 6155
Kirkland, WA 98034
(800) 456-0234 Orders
(206) 823-8198 Information
(206) 823-6204 FAX

Kuma Computers Ltd.,   Macintosh
12 Horseshoe Park,   IBM
Pangbourne,
Berks RG8 7JW
0734 844335 TEL   EPS: Variable
0734 844339 FAX

We at 3G Graphics make every effort to bring a fresh, unique approach to our clip art because we care about improving the quality of your printed piece, says Gail Giaimo (President) and Glenn Giaimo (Vice President) of **3G Graphics**. 3G offers two contemporary clip-art collections called *Images With Impact!™*

- Graphics and Symbols 1
- Business 1

Both collections are available for Mac and IBM computers and include ideas for using the art in a variety of applications.

Many of 3G's images were created by layering different graphic elements. These elements can be separated (ungrouped) by using either Aldus Freehand™ or Adobe Illustrator®. Separating the elements significantly increases the size of the clip-art collection. *The image count that we give for the clip-art packages does not include separating the images.*

Macintosh System Requirements

- PostScript printer or typesetter.
- 1 Meg RAM (2 megs recommended).
- One 800K disk drive.
- Program that can read *.EPS* files.

IBM System Requirements

- PostScript printer or typesetter.
- 640K RAM (1.2 megs recommended).
- One high density 5.25-inch (3.5-inch disks available upon request).
- Program that can read *.EPS* files.

Images With Impact!™
Graphics and Symbols 1
(80 images)

Images with Impact!™
Business 1
(142 images)

Archive Arts

Archive Arts
P.O. Box 39522
Downey, CA 90241
(213) 861-7562

Kuma Computers Ltd.,
12 Horseshoe Park,
Pangbourne,
Berks RG8 7JW
0734 844335 TEL   Mac: TIFF
0734 844339 FAX   IBM: PCX/TIF

Macintosh
IBM

300 dpi
300 dpi

Archive Arts specializes in creating clip-art from the illustrations of European and American graphic designers of the 18th, 19th, and early 20th centuries. Illustrations are taken from 60-200 year old publications and saved in the .TIFF, .PCX, and .TIF formats. All collections are available for both Macintosh and IBM computers. The company also offers a subject search service.

Shown on the following pages are samples from two Archive Arts[1] collections.

- Sampler collection.
- Old Fashioned Christmas collection.

Macintosh Systems Requirements

- One 800K disk drive.

IBM System Requirements

- No special requirements.

---

[1] *Archive Arts* only provided the author with two complete clip-art packages. For this reason, only two of their collections are shown.

Archive Arts
Sampler Disk
(15 images)

Archive Arts
Old Fashioned Christmas Edition
(49 images)

MERRY CHRISTMAS

DISC

Devonian International
Software Company
P. O. Box 2351
Montclair, CA 91763
(818) 700-9525

Kuma Computers Ltd.,
12 Horseshoe Park,   Macintosh
Pangbourne,
Berks RG8 7JW   Paint: 75 dpi
0734 844335 TEL
0734 844339 FAX

Devonian International Software Company was founded in 1985 by Dr. Elliot Weinstein--a practicing pediatrician--and Mr. Glenn Mitchell, a manufacturing engineer in the aerospace industry. DISC designs fonts and clip-art. They also offer a service that converts company logos to a font.

Devonia itself is a fictional country named after Devonshire, England. The *Devonian International Cookbook* is available from DISC and features recipes, folklore, and history about Devonia.

Devonian publishes one collection of clip-art which is called *ARTagenix: Planes of Fame*. This collection features clip-art of modern U.S. military aircraft.

Macintosh System Requirements

* No special requirements.

229

ARTagenix™
Planes of Fame
(535 images)

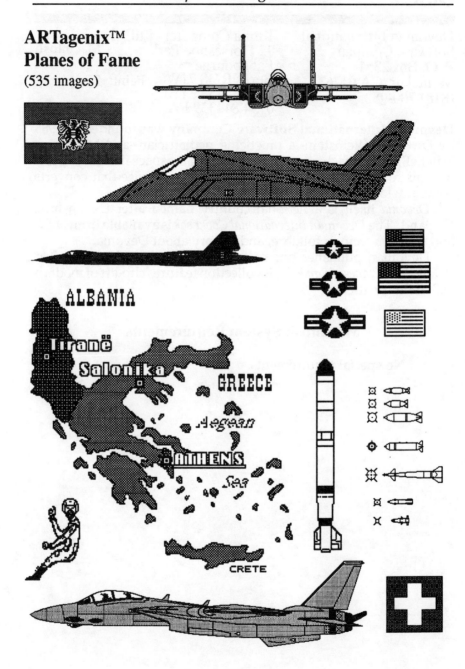

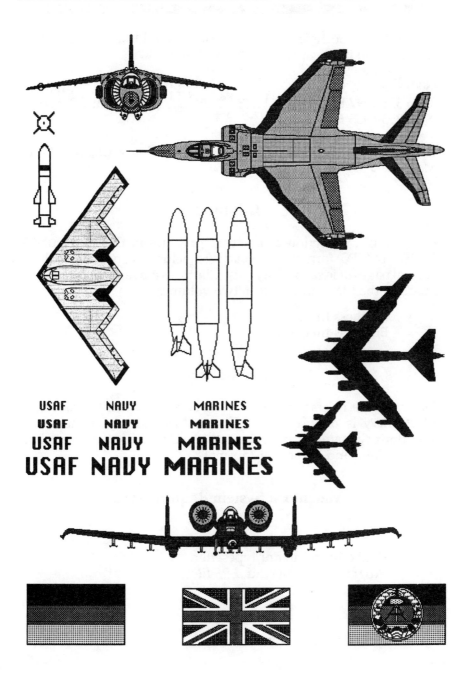

USAF USAF **USAF** **USAF**

NAVY NAVY **NAVY** **NAVY**

MARINES MARINES **MARINES** **MARINES**

231

Dream Maker

Dream Maker Software
7217 Foothill Boulevard
Tujunga, CA 91402
(800) 876-5665 Orders
(818) 353-2297 Business
(818) 353-6988 Fax

Kuma Computers Ltd.,
12 Horseshoe Park,
Pangbourne,
Berks RG8 7JW
0734 844335 TEL
0734 844339 FAX

Macintosh
IBM

EPS: Variable
Paint: 72 dpi

Dream Maker Software™ has two clip-art lines: *Cliptures*™ and *MacGallery*™.

Cliptures

Cliptures is a collection of business graphics in the encapsulated PostScript (EPS) format. Each package includes a booklet which has several pages of ideas and layouts. Cliptures is available for both the Mac and the IBM computers in two volumes.

- Business Images 1
- Business Images 2

MacGallery

Dream Maker refers to the *MacGallery* clip-art as their *fun* collection. MacGallery is only available for the Macintosh and includes a selection of general purpose clip-art. MacGallery is available in both the MacPaint and HyperCard formats.

Macintosh System Requirements

Cliptures

- PostScript printer or typesetter.
- Program that can read *.EPS* files.

MacGallery, MacPaint version

- No special requirements.

MacGallery, Hypercard version

- PostScript printer or typesetter.
- Mac Plus or higher.
- Two 800K disk drives (hard disk recommended).
- *HyperCard or HyperDA™*.

IBM System Requirements

Cliptures

- PostScript printer or typesetter.
- IBM-compatible computer (286 or 386 recommended).
- One 5.25-inch disk drive.[1]

MacGallery, Hypercard version

- Apple Hypercard program.

---

[1] If your original order specifies 3.5-inch diskettes, they are provided without additional charge. If you exchange your 5.25-inch disks for 3.5-inch disks after receiving the clip-art, there is a $20 handling fee.

Cliptures™
Business Images Volume 1
(139 images)

Cliptures™
Business Images Volume 2
(206 images)

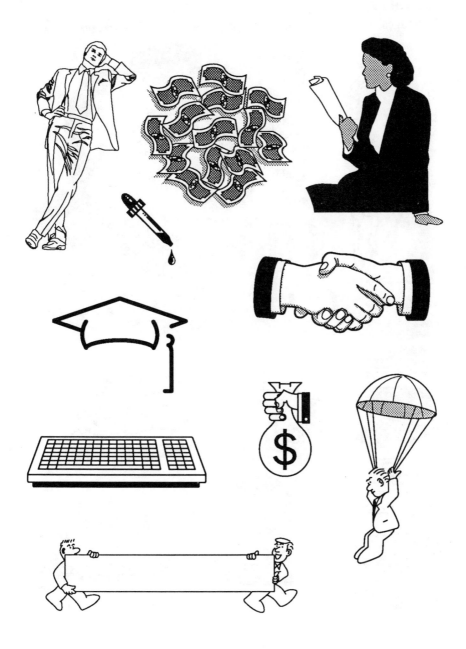

MacGallery™
(535 images)

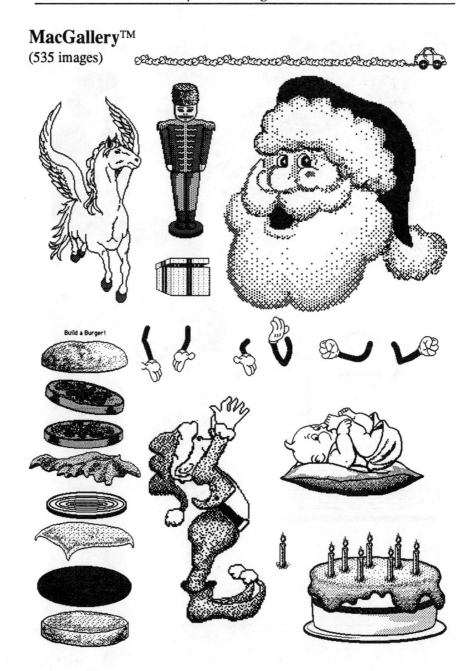

Build a Burger!

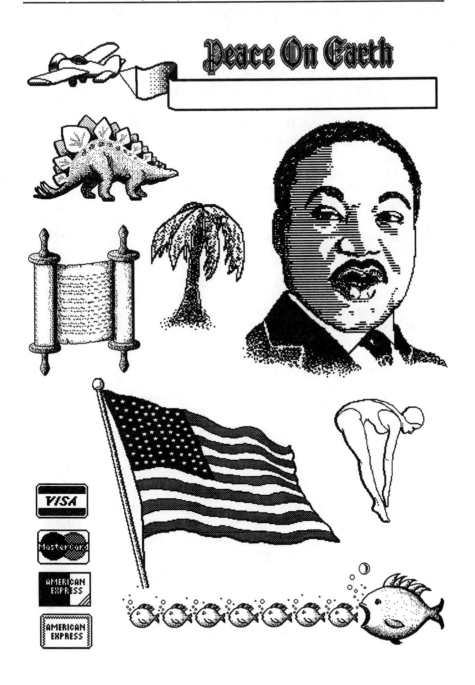

Peace On Earth

Dubl-Click

Dubl-Click Software, Inc.
9316 Deering Avenue
Chatsworth, CA 91311
(818) 700-9525

Kuma Computers Ltd.,
12 Horseshoe Park,
Pangbourne,
Berks RG8 7JW
0734 844335 TEL
0734 844339 FAX

Macintosh

EPS: Variable
Paint: 72 dpi

Dubl-Click Software, Inc. was founded in 1985 by Cliff Joyce, a graphic designer, and Austin Durbin, an assembly language programmer.

Dubl-Click calls their clip-art collections *WetPaint™*. Each of their nine collections is available in the MacPaint format and includes a detailed instruction manual.

WetPaint collections include hundreds of images designed for both home and business use. Samples from each collection begin on page 242 and include

- All the People
- Animal Kingdom
- Classic Clip-Art
- For Publishing
- Industrial Revolution
- Island Life
- Old Earth Almanac
- Printer's Helper
- Special Occasions

Dubl-Click provides two desk accessories (free of charge) with each WetPaint clip-art collection. Instructions for installing and using the accessories is included in the user manual that comes with each WetPaint collection.

- *ArtRoundup™* is a program that lets you view, copy, and manipulate Paint files without using a Paint program. ArtRoundup also has a *slideshow* feature that lets you look at files without having to open and close each one.

    ArtRoundup's tools include lasso, marquee, grabber, eraser, pencil, and an assortment of slideshow controls. *ArtRoundup requires at least a Macintosh 512E with System 4.1.*

- *PatternMover™* lets you design and edit patterns, and move patterns from one Paint file to another. PatternMover includes a variety of tools including a random pattern generator.

Dubl-Click's other products and services include

- *World Class LaserType*, nine PostScript font collections for PostScript printers. (See the samples beginning on page 200.)

- *World Class Fonts*, four collections of bit-mapped fonts for dot matrix printers.

- *MacTut/ProGlyph*, a collection of hieroglyphic fonts and ancient Egyptian clip-art.

- *Logos On Line*, a service that converts a logo to a PostScript font.

Macintosh System Requirements

- One 800K disk drive (hard disk recommended).

Wetpaint™
All The People
(1808 images)

Wetpaint™
Animal Kingdom
(333 images)

Wetpaint™
Classic Clip-Art
(2121 images)

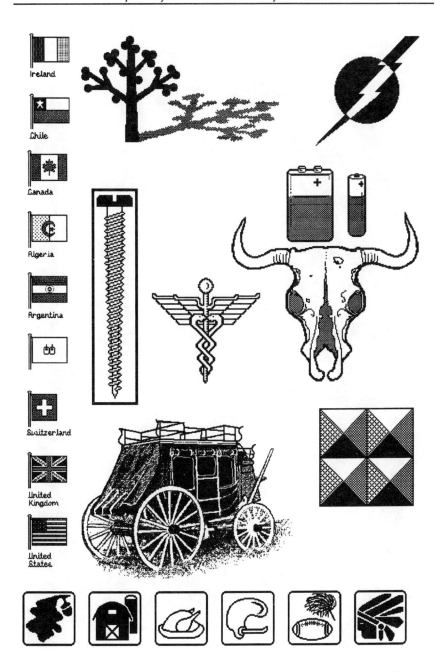

Ireland

Chile

Canada

Algeria

Argentina

Switzerland

United
Kingdom

United
States

Wetpaint™
For Publishing
(968 images)

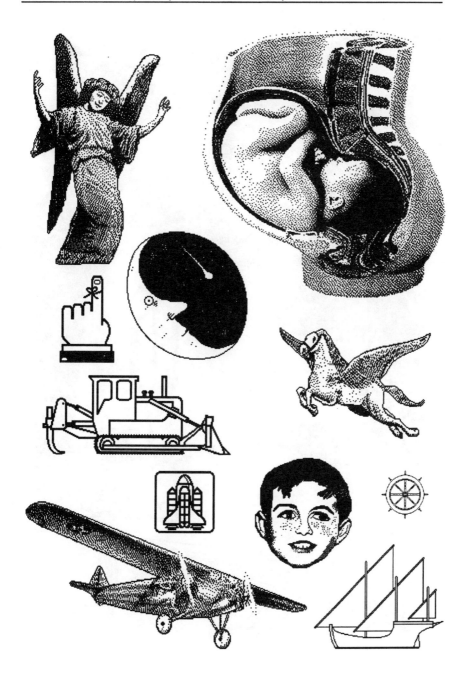

249

Wetpaint™
Industrial Revolution
(697 images)

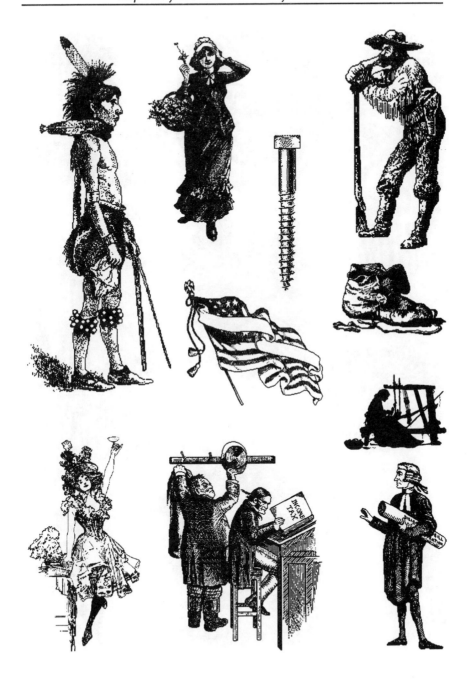

Wetpaint™
Island Life
(361 images)

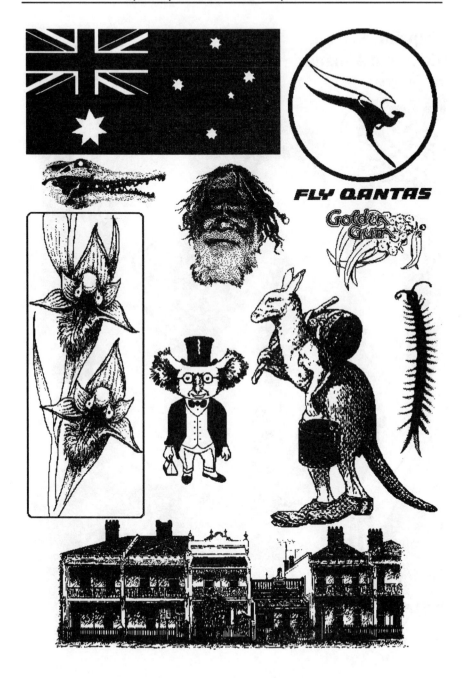

FLY QANTAS

Golden Gum

Wetpaint™
Old Earth Almanac
(361 images)

Sequoia

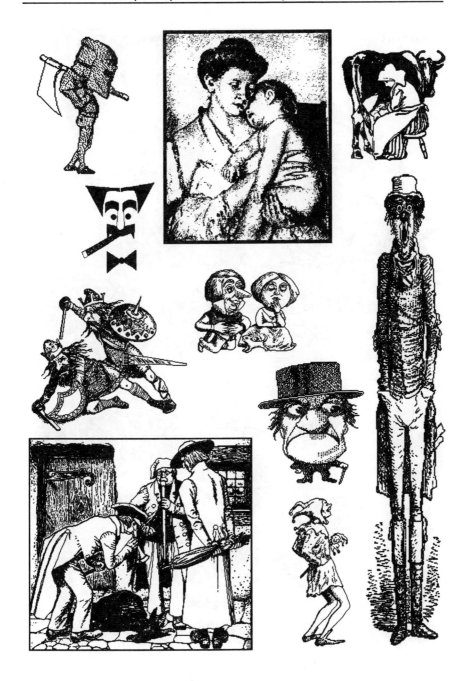

255

Wetpaint™
Printer's Helper
(395 images)

Wetpaint™
Special Occasions
(285 images)

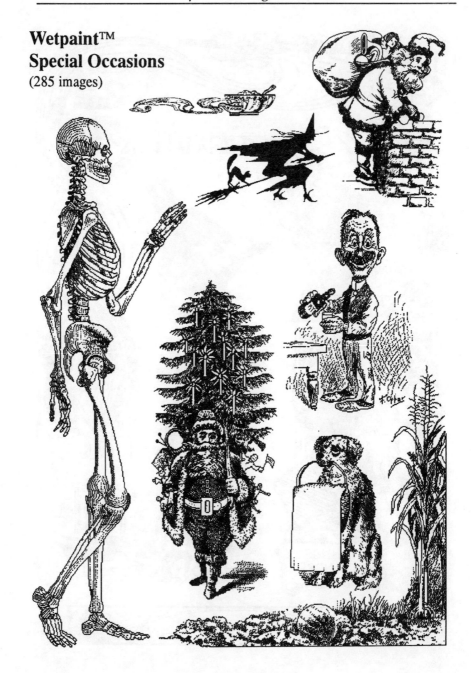

Dynamic Graphics

Dynamic Graphics, Inc
6000 N. Forest Park Drive
Peoria, IL 61614
(800) 255-8800
Dynamic Graphics UK Ltd
Media House, Eastways Ind. Park
Whitham, Essex, CM8 3YJ
0376 516006

Macintosh
IBM

Mac: Paint	300 dpi
IBM: PCX	300 dpi

Dynamic Graphics, Inc. is one of the world's leading creators and publishers of camera-ready art. They offer electronic art, print art, books, reference materials, training, and related services to the graphic arts industry. Incorporated in 1964, Dynamic Graphics currently distributes products in over eighty countries.

Dynamic Graphics offers some of their electronic art collections in EPS (Encapsulated PostScript) format and other electronic art collections in non-EPS formats. All collections are available for both Macintosh and IBM computers. Each collection is accompanied by an idea booklet with sample designs.

DeskTop Art® /EPS

Dynamics Graphics offers a continually expanding selection of electronic art collections in the EPS format. Each collection contains 38-50 full-page images. Collections may be purchased separately or by subscription to Dynamic Graphics' *Designer's Club*.

- Athletics 1
- Design Elements 1
- Potpourri 1
- School Days 1

- Commerce 1
- People 1
- Sales & Promotions 1
- Seasonal 1

DeskTop Art® (non-EPS images)

Dynamic Graphics offers eight electronic art collections that are not in the EPS format. These collections include 131-216 images. There are 3-9 images per page. These collections include

- Artfolio 1
- Business 1
- Four Seasons 1
- Health Care 1

- Borders & Mortices 1
- Education 1
- Graphic & Symbols 1
- Sports 1

260

Macintosh System Requirements

EPS Collections

- PostScript printer or typesetter.
- 1 Meg RAM (2 megs recommended with *Adobe Illustrator 88*).
- One 800K disk drive.
- Program that can read *.EPS* files.

Paint Collections

- No special requirements.

IBM System Requirements

EPS Collections

- PostScript printer or typesetter.
- 640K RAM (1.2 megs expanded memory recommended).
- One high-density disk drive.
- Program that can read *.EPS* files.

Non-EPS Collections

- 640K RAM (1.2 megs expanded memory recommended).

DeskTop Art®
Athletics 1
(40 images)

DeskTop Art®
Commerce 1
(46 images)

DeskTop Art®
Design Elements 1
(46 images)

**DeskTop Art®
People 1**
(38 images)

**DeskTop Art®
Potpourri 1**
(46 images)

DeskTop Art®
Sales & Promotions 1
(46 images)

DeskTop Art®
School Days 1
(44 images)

DeskTop Art®
Seasonal 1
(44 images)

DeskTop Art®
Artfolio 1
(191 images)

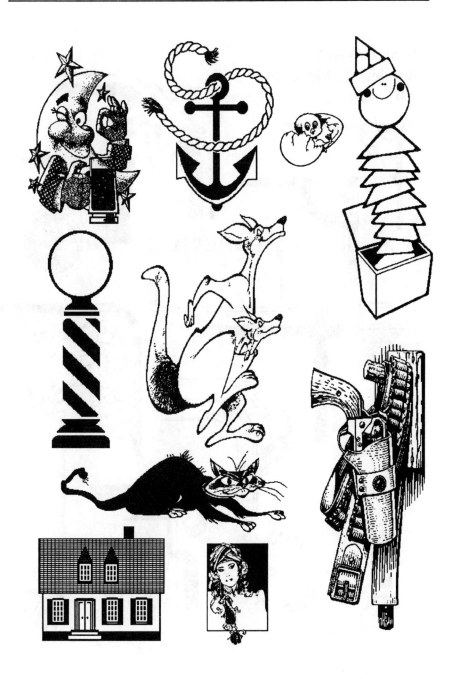

DeskTop Art®
Borders & Mortices 1
(131 images)

DeskTop Art®
Business 1
(201 images)

DeskTop Art®
Education 1
(201 images)

DeskTop Art®
Four Seasons 1
(201 images)

DeskTop Art®
Graphics & Symbols 1
(216 images)

DeskTop Art®
Health Care 1
(201 images)

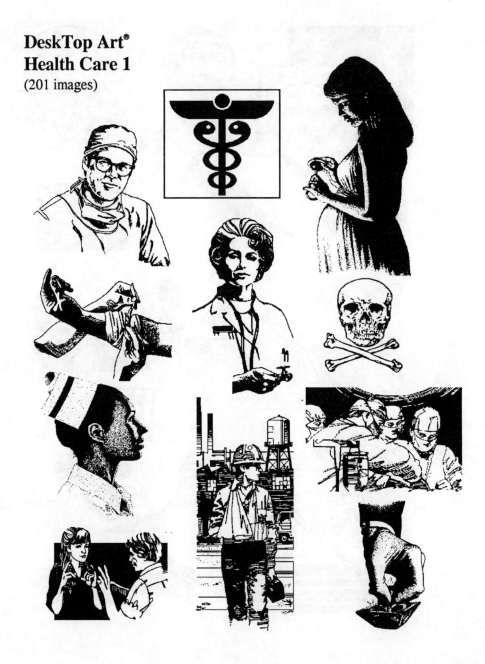

283

DeskTop Art®
Sports 1
(199 images)

Eykon

Eykon Computer Graphics
P.O. Box 2142
Round Rock, Texas 78680
(512) 388-7099

Phone Kuma for latest details

0734 844335

Macintosh
IBM

Mac:	EPS	Variable
	Paint	72 dpi
	PICT/TIFF	300 dpi
IBM:	EPS	Variable
	IMG/PCX/	
	TIF	300 dpi

Our desire is to supply quality electronic art at a competitive price for everyone's presentation graphics and desktop publishing needs, says Jeff Hancock of **Eykon Computer Graphics**.

Eykon produces electronic art for Macintosh, Apple, IBM, and Atari ST computers. All clip-art is *archived* (saved in a compressed form) and must be *extracted* (removed from archived form) using a program that Eykon provides.

Image Works

Eykon's electronic art collection is called *Image Works*. *Image Works* is organized into three levels: Series, Categories, and Images. Each *series* is comprised of one or more categories of images.

Eykon's clip-art may be purchased by series, by category, by individual image, or in its entirety.

Image Works series and categories are listed below. Samples of the clip-art begin on page 288.

- **Antics Series.**
  Categories: Communication Antics, Seasonal Silhouettes.

- **Cartoon Mania Series.**
  Categories: Computer, Dinosaur, Jelly Bean, Penguin, Potato.

- **Decorative Designs.**
  Category: Decorative Flora.

- **Equestrian.**

286

- **Humor Series.**
  Categories: Business, Educational, Medical, Religious, Sports.

- **Precision Portfolio.**
  Categories: Education, Greeting Cards, Hands, People Silhouettes, Special Occasions.

- **Studio Editions.**
  Category: Business graphics.

Macintosh System Requirements

- No special requirements.

IBM System Requirements

- No special requirements.

Image Works
Antics Series
(54 images)

Image Works
Cartoon Mania Series
(66 images)

Image Works
Decorative Designs
(27 images)

**Image Works
Equestrian**
(26 images)

Image Works
Humor Series
(126 images)

Image Works
Precision Portfolio
(101 images)

"Exhausted"

Image Works
Studio Editions
(30 images)

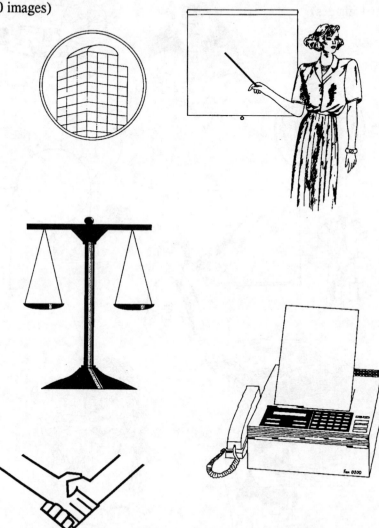

MGI

Marketing Graphics, Inc.
4401 Dominion Boulevard
Suite 210
Glen Allen VA 23060
(804) 747 6991

Kuma Computers Ltd
12 Horseshoe PArk
Pangbourne
Berks RG8 7JW
0734 844335

Macintosh
IBM

Mac:	Paint	72 dpi
	PICT	300 dpi
IBM:	PCX/CGM	300 dpi

Marketing Graphics, Inc. (MGI) specializes in computer-generated graphic products. MGI was established in 1985 and now markets its products worldwide.

MGI's electronic-art libraries are called *PicturePaks*™ and are designed primarily for business publications and presentations. All PicturePak editions are available for both Mac and IBM computers.

PicturePak editions for the Mac include clip-art in both the *Paint* and *PICT* formats. PicturePak editions for IBM computers include clip-art in both the *CGM* and *PCC* (*PCX*) formats. Each PicturePak edition has a reference manual with tips on using the clip-art with several popular software programs. The PicturePak line is divided into two series.

- **Eye Openers Series.**
  Editions: Finance and Administration, Executive and Management, Sales and Marketing.

- **USA Series.**
  Edition: Federal Government.

Several PicturePak editions are also available for demonstration software packages such as *Storyboard, Show Partner*, and *VideoShow*.

Macintosh System Requirements

- No special requirements.

IBM System Requirements

- No special requirements.

PicturePak™
Executive & Management Edition
(180 images)

Challenge

PicturePak™
Finance & Administration Edition
(180 images)

PicturePak™
Sales & Meetings Edition
(180 images)

PicturePak™
Federal Government Edition
(169 images)

VETO

Metro ImageBase

Metro ImageBase Inc.	Resolution Systems Plc.,	Macintosh
18623 Ventura B'vard,	Lombard House,	IBM
Suite 210,	2 Purley Way,	
Tarzana, CA 91356	Croydon CR0 3JP	
(818)997-8811	081 665 5050 TEL	Mac: TIFF 300 dpi
	081 665 5220 FAX	IBM: PCX/TIF 300 dpi

Metro ImageBase™, Inc. is a division of Metro Creative Graphics, a leading supplier of advertising art for newspapers since 1910. Metro ImageBase has selected images from its extensive clip-art library and made them available in electronic form for both Macintosh and IBM computers.

All of Metro ImageBase's electronic-art is *archived* (saved in a compressed form) and must be *extracted* (removed from archived form) using a program that Metro ImageBase provides. Detailed instructions for using the program are provided in the user manual that comes with each of Metro ImageBase's fourteen collections.

- Art Deco
- Borders and Boxes
- Business Graphics
- Computers & Technology
- Exercise and Fitness
- Food
- The Four Seasons
- Newsletter Maker
- Nine to Five
- People
- ReportMaker
- Team Sports
- Travel
- Weekend Sports

Macintosh System Requirements

- Hard disk.

IBM System Requirements

- Hard disk with 1.5 meg free space.
- DOS 3.1 or higher.

Electronic Art
Art Deco
(101 images)

Electronic Art
Borders and Boxes
(100 images)

Electronic Art
Business Graphics
(100 images)

Electronic Art
Computers and Technology
(100 images)

Electronic Art
Exercise and Fitness
(100 images)

Electronic Art
Food
(100 images)

Electronic Art
The Four Seasons
(100 images)

Electronic Art
NewsLetter Maker
(100 images)

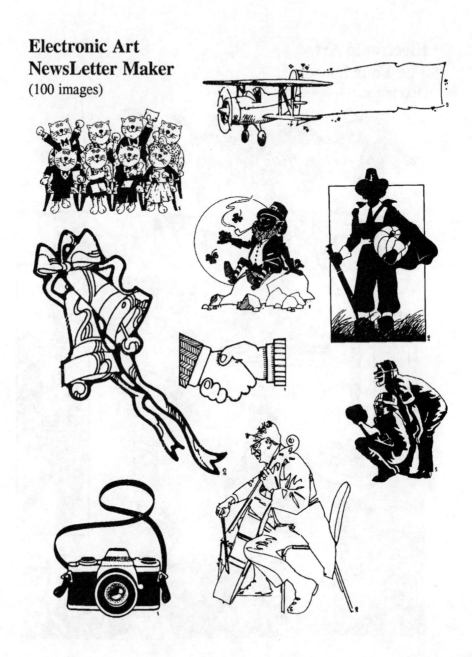

**Electronic Art
Nine to Five**
(100 images)

**Electronic Art
People**
(100 images)

Electronic Art
ReportMaker
(100 images)

Electronic Art
Team Sports
(100 images)

**Electronic Art
Travel**
(100 images)

Electronic Art
Weekend Sports
(100 images)

Multi-Ad

Multi-Ad Services, Inc.™
1720 West Detweiller Drive
Peoria, IL 61615
(800) 447-1950
(309) 692-8378 (FAX)

Studio Box Ltd.,
51 Southampton Rd,
Reading,
Berks
0734 502556 TEL
0734 573935 FAX

Macintosh
IBM

EPS: Variable

Multi-Ad Services, Inc.™ is an employee-owned company with over 300 people. Founded in 1946, Multi-Ad provides a variety of products and services to the advertising community.

Multi-Ad's *ProArt Professional Art Library™* was designed to meet the needs of corporate communication departments and advertising agencies. ProArt is comprised of six collections. Three of the collections are available for both Mac and IBM computers; the other three are only available for the Mac. ProArt collections are available on diskette and CD (compact disc). ProArt collections include

- Business (Mac & IBM).
- Holiday (Mac & IBM).
- Sports (Mac & IBM).
- Border & Heading (Mac only).
- Food (Mac only).
- People (Mac only).

ProArt is only one of Multi-Ad's graphic-related products and services. Others include

- **Ad-Builder® Electronic.** Ad-Builder is a monthly, retail-art service. Provided primarily to newspapers, this service offers art and ideas for advertisements, radio scripts, point-of-purchase displays, and sales and training. Ad-Builder is available in both print form and on CD.

- **SCAN®.** Similar to *Ad-Builder Electronic*, SCAN is also an art subscription service geared to newspapers. SCAN offers clip-art that focuses on the real estate, automotive, and employment markets. SCAN is available in both print form and on CD.

- **Commercial Binder & Print**, a service that provides printed binders and tabs, color separations, pre-press production, and silk screening.

- **Kwikee® Illustration System.** Kwikee is a collection of print clip-art of products from major US food manufacturers. Kwikee is distributed free of charge to advertising chains and supermarkets. Other Kwikee systems exist for other markets including Mass Merchandising, Automotive, and Toy & Games.
- **Multi-Ad Creator™.** Creator is a program designed for ad layout and composition. Creator is available for Macintosh computers.

Macintosh System Requirements

- PostScript printer or typesetter.
- Program that can read *.EPS* files.

IBM System Requirements

- PostScript printer or typesetter.
- Program that can read *.EPS* files.

ProArt
The Business Collection
(132 images)

ProArt
The Holiday Collection
(118 images)

ProArt
The Sports Collection
(108 images)

ProArt
The Border & Heading Collection
(100 images)

ProArt
The Food Collection
(100 images)

ProArt
The People Collection
(100 images)

One Mile Up

One Mile Up, Inc.
7011 Evergreen Court
Annandale, VA 22003
(703) 642-1177

Phone Kuma for latest details

0734 844335

Macintosh
IBM

EPS: Variable

Founded in 1987, **One Mile Up, Inc.** specializes in clip-art images for the United States government, the Department of Defense, and contractors doing business with the federal government.

One Mile Up has one collection of clip-art which the company calls *Federal Clip Art*. Federal Clip Art is available for Macintosh, IBM (MS-DOS), and UNIX-based computers.

In addition to the clip-art provided in the package, the purchaser is invited to select and send away for five additional images which are provided without charge. The purchaser may select from a variety of illustrations such as government leaders, computers, and the emblems and seals of various United States government agencies and departments.[1]

Macintosh System Requirements

- PostScript printer or typesetter.
- 800K disk drive (hard disk recommended).
- One Meg RAM (more memory recommended).
- Program that can read .*EPS* files.

IBM System Requirements

- PostScript printer or typesetter.
- Program that can read .*EPS* files.

---

[1] One Mile Up provides seals and emblems of the United States government. The use of some illustrations is regulated by federal law. Misuse of these illustrations may be punishable by fine and/or imprisonment.

Federal Clip Art™
(159 images)

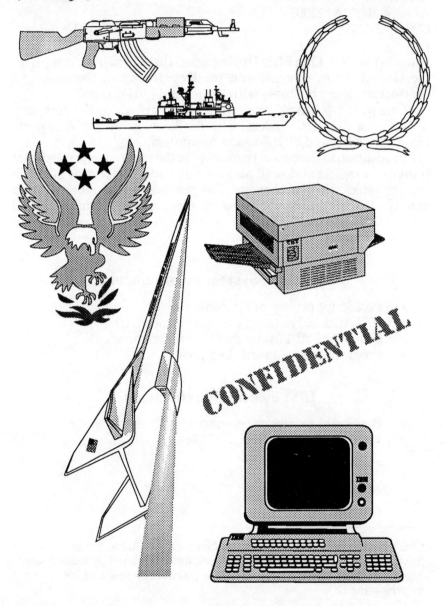

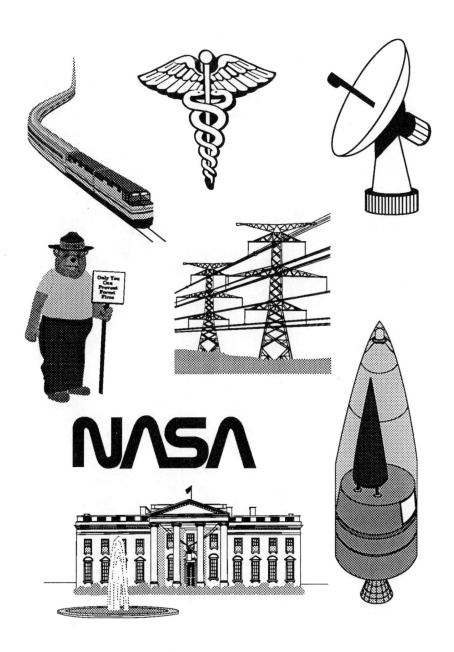

330

Qualitas

Qualitas Trading Company
6907 Norfold Road
Berkeley, CA 94705
(415) 848-8080

Kuma Computers Ltd.,
12 Horseshoe Park,
Pangbourne,
Berks RG8 7JW
0734 844335 TEL

Macintosh

Paint: 72 dpi

Qualitas Trading Company distributes several clip art packages of oriental clip-art and designs for the Enzan-Hoshigumi Company, Ltd., of Tokyo, Japan. Each of Qualitas' three products comes with a user's guide that describes the different Japanese characters and illustrations.

- Scroll I: Heaven.

- Scroll II: Earth.

- "Borders" Scroll.

Qualitas also markets *MacCalligraphy*, a mouse-driven draw program that simulates drawing and writing on absorbent rice paper. *MacCalligraphy* requires a Macintosh with at least 512K of memory.

Macintosh System Requirements

- No special requirements.

Japanese Clip Art™
Scroll I: "Heaven"
(315 images)

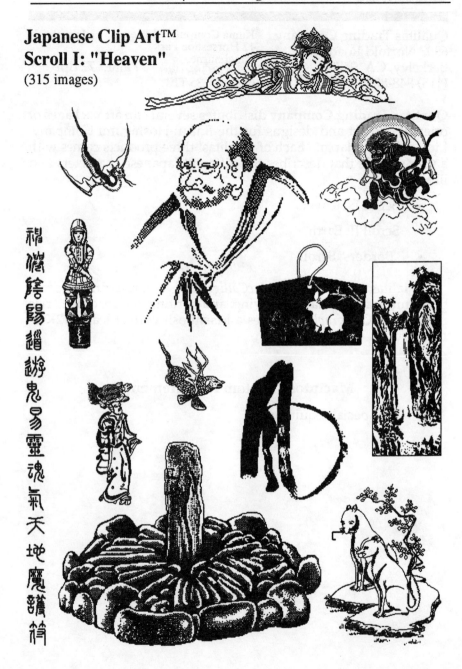

Japanese Clip Art™
Scroll II "Earth"
(340 images)

Japanese Clip Art™
"Borders" Scroll
(402 images)

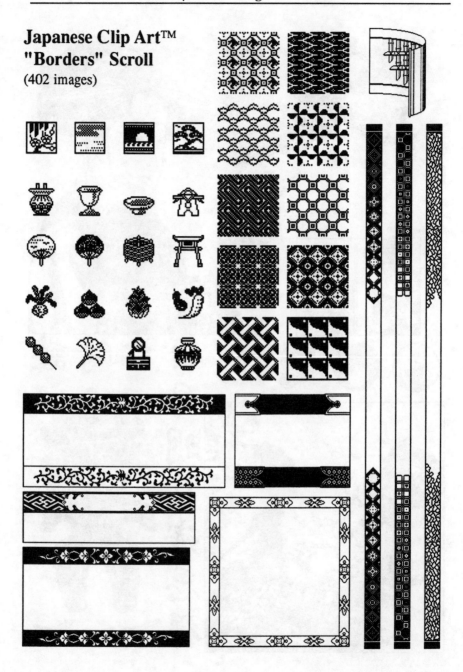

Silicon Designs

Silicon Designs
P.O. Box 2234
Orinda, CA 94563
(415) 254-1460

Macintosh

EPS: Variable

Silicon Designs specializes in computerized graphic-design and typesetting services for the Macintosh. Founded in May 1987, Silicon Designs offers one clip-art collection in what is to become their *Masterworks™* series.

The first clip-art collection in the Masterworks series is *Art Nouveau Images*. Art Nouveau Images is a collection of clip-art designs that have been recreated from popular art pieces of the late nineteenth and early twentieth centuries. A brochure that comes with the clip-art explains the history of each image and details on how each image was recreated.

Macintosh Systems - Hardware Requirements

- PostScript printer or typesetter.
- One 800K disk drive.
- 1 Meg RAM.
- Program that can read *.EPS* files.

Art Nouveau Images
(12 images)

Studio Advertising Art

Studio Advertising Art
4305 East Sahara Ave. #1
Las Vegas, NV 89104
(702) 641-7041

Kuma Computers Ltd.,
12 Horseshoe Park,
Pangbourne,
Berks RG8 7JW
0734 844335 TEL
0734 844339 FAX

Macintosh
IBM

EPS: Variable

Excellence in advertising is what **Studio Advertising Art** says was the motivating factor behind their establishment. Established in 1984, Studio Advertising Art designed graphics for advertising. In 1987, the company began designing electronic art for use by graphic art studios, individuals, companies, and professional publishers.

Studio Advertising Art releases new clip-art collections every quarter as part of their *Click & Clip* series. Each collection is composed of new images created by the company's in-house art department.

Click & Clip collections may be purchased separately or as part of Studio Advertising Art's subscription service. All collections are available for both Macintosh and IBM computers.

- Winter 1987
- Spring 1988
- Summer 1988
- Fall 1988
- Winter 1988
- Spring 1989
- Summer 1989

- Fall 1989
- Special Issue 1.0
- Click and Clip 500
- Military Art 1.1
- Medical Health
- Road & Warning Signs

Macintosh System Requirements

- PostScript printer or typesetter.
- Programs that can read *EPS* files.

IBM System Requirements

- PostScript printer or typesetter.
- Programs that can read *.EPS* files.

Click & Clip
Winter Issue 1987
(50 images)

Click & Clip
Spring Issue 1988
(50 images)

Click & Clip
Summer Issue 1988
(49 images)

Click & Clip
Fall Issue 1988
(50 images)

Click & Clip
Winter Issue 1988
(50 images)

Click & Clip
Spring Issue 1989
(50 images)

Click & Clip
Summer Issue 1989
(50 images)

Click & Clip
Fall 1989
(51 images)

Click & Clip
Special Issue 1.0
(20 images)

Click & Clip
500 Illustrations
(503 images)

FORECAST

Grand Opening

Click & Clip
Military Art 1.1
(147 images)

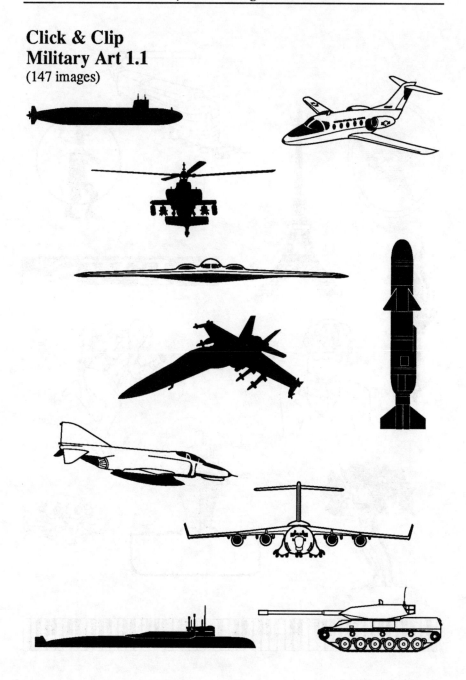

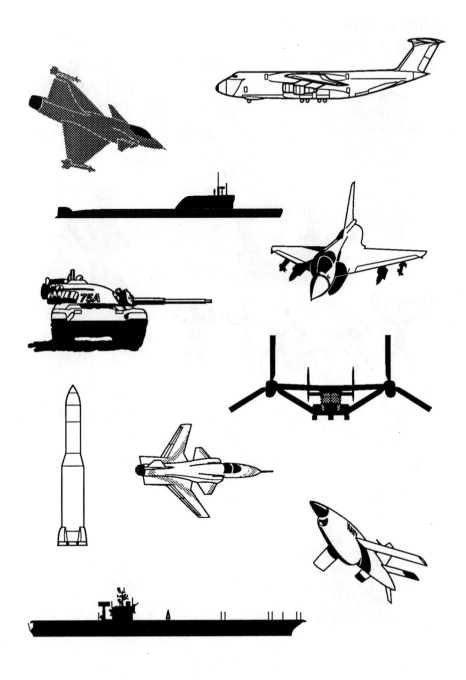

Click & Clip
Medical Health
(110 images)

Click & Clip
Road & Warning Signs
(105 images)

T/Maker

	Persona, Unit1		
T/Maker Co.	Silver Glade Bus park,		Macintosh
1390 Villa St,	Leatherhead Rd,		IBM
Mountain View,	Chessington,		
CA 94041	Surrey KT9 2NQ		
(415)962-0195	03727 29611 TEL	Mac: EPS	Variable
(415)962-0201 FAX	03727 43535 FAX	Paint	72 dpi
		IBM: EPS	Variable
		GEM/PCX	72 dpi
		MSP/PCX	72 dpi

T/Maker Company is dedicated to developing and shipping graphic-oriented products. Founded in 1979, T/Maker is credited with producing one of the first software products for the Macintosh *(Personal Graphics)*.

T/Maker has seven clip-art collections which the company refers to as *ClickArt®*. Each collection is available for both Macintosh and IBM computers. Different collections are offered in various formats for each of the two systems. A detailed user manual and index is included with each collection.

EPS Collections

Two of T/Maker's collections are offered in the *.EPS* format. Each collection includes over 180 images. Some are a full-page in size.

- Business Art.
- EPS Illustrations.

Non-EPS Collections

T/Maker offers five ClickArt collections in non-EPS formats.

- Business Images.
- Christian Images.
- Holidays.
- Personal Graphics.
- Publications.

Collections for the Macintosh are supplied in both MacPaint and HyperCard Stackware formats and include a free copy of *ClipOut* (see below).

Collections for the IBM are available in either GEM/PCX or MSP/PCX (Windows) format. *Note: The GEM format of some portfolios contains fewer images.*

Other Products

In addition to ClickArt, T/Maker offers other graphic-oriented products just for the Macintosh.

- **LaserLetters.** LaserLetters is T/Maker's line of laser fonts for PostScript printers. (See page 210 for more information.)

- **ClipOut.** ClipOut is a painting and organization tool that lets you access MacPaint files without leaving your current program. ClipOut is included free with all non-EPS art collections for the Macintosh.

- **Effects.** Effects is a tool which lets you rotate, slant, distort, or change the perspective of graphic images.

Macintosh System Requirements

EPS Collections

- PostScript printer or typesetter.
- One 800K disk drive.
- Programs which can read *EPS* files.

Non-EPS Collections

- No special requirements.

IBM System Requirements

EPS Collections

- PostScript printer or typesetter.
- Programs which can read *.EPS* files.

Non-EPS Collections

- No special requirements.

357

ClickArt® /EPS
Business Art
(220 images)

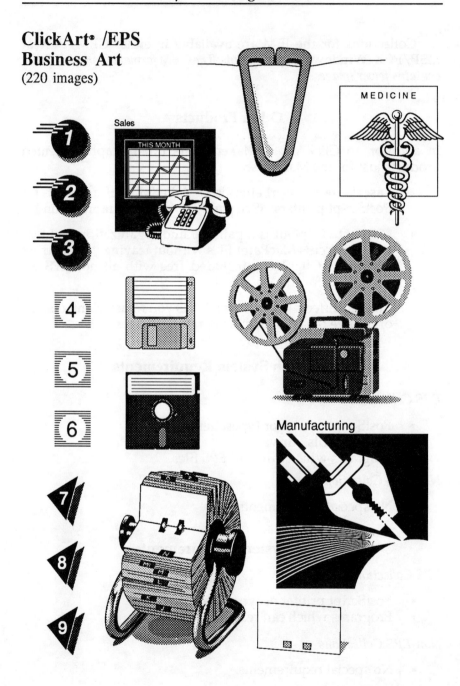

ClickArt®/EPS
Illustrations
(177 images)

ANNOUNCEMENTS

ClickArt®
Business Images
(1,246 images)

363

ClickArt®
Christian Images
(602 images)

ClickArt®
Holidays
(251 images)

Happy
Mother's Day

Happy
Hanukkah

367

ClickArt®
Personal Graphics
(139 images)

7 Appendix

Foreign Language Fonts

Many foreign language fonts are available for the Macintosh. Unfortunately, few foreign languages are available in PostScript. Those fonts that are available in PostScript are marked below with an asterisk (*).

Most foreign-language fonts are bit-mapped fonts designed to work with dot matrix printers. Although you may use any of the bit-mapped fonts on your PostScript laser printer, expect significantly lower resolution (72 dpi) than when using a PostScript font (300⁺ dpi).

The list below is in alphabetical order by foreign language (left-most column). A list of font company addresses and phone numbers appears at the end of the *Appendix*.

Language	Font Name	Font Company
Arabic	Riyady	Devonian
Ancient Aramaic	Arpad	Devonian
Armenian	Yerevan	Devonian
Bohemian	Prague	Devonian
Cyrillic[1]	Vladivostok	Devonian

---

[1] For use with Russian, Ukrainian, White Russian, Bulgarian, and Serbian.

370

Language	Font Name	Font Company
Czech	Prague	Devonian
Devonian	Trizekh	Devonian
East European	Prague	Devonian
Esperanto	Trizekh	Devonian
Finnish	Budapest	Devonian
Gaelic	Limerick	Devonian
German	Dusseldorf	Devonian
Greek	Athens	Dubl-Click
Greek (light style)	Delphi	Devonian
Greek (heavy style)	Sparta	Devonian
Hebrew	Tel Aviv	Devonian
Hebrew*	Tel Aviv	Devonian
Hebrew (cursive)	Haifa	Devonian
Hungarian	Budapest	Devonian
Korean	Seoul	Devonian
Laotian	Luang Phrabang	Devonian
Latin[1]	Lunaria	Devonian
Minoan-Cretan[2]	Mycenae	Devonian
Persian Cuneiform	Persepolis	Devonian
Polish	Prague	Devonian
Romanian	Prague	Devonian
Russian Cyrillic*[3]	Sverdlovsk	Devonian
Turkish	Budapest	Devonian
Slovak	Prague	Devonian
Slovenian	Prague	Devonian
Thai	Bangkok	Devonian

[1] Designed for languages using a modified Latin-based alphabet.

[2] Linear B syllabary.

[3] For use with Russian, Old Russian, Serbian, Ukrainian, Byelorussian, Macedonian, and others.

Symbol Fonts

Several companies offer a variety of symbol fonts for the Mac. Unlike foreign language fonts, most symbol fonts are available for PostScript printers. Those that are only available for dot matrix are marked below with a section mark (§).

The fonts below are listed in alphabetical order by subject matter (left-most column). A list of font company addresses and phone numbers appears at the end of the *Appendix*.

Symbol Subject	Font Name	Company
Alphabet[1]	ASCII City	Dubl-Click
Alphabet§[2]	Overstrike	Dubl-Click
Alphabet Keys[3]	PIXymbols 2012	Page Studio
Agriculture	PIXymbols 5002	Page Studio
Architectural Symbols§	Tempe	Dubl-Click
Arrows	ArrowDynamic	EmDash
	BulletsNstuff	EmDash
Arrows (bold)	ArrowDynamic Bold	EmDash
Arrows (heavy)	ArrowDynamic Heavy	EmDash
Art Deco[4]	PIXymbols 8062	Page Studio
Astrological[5]	PIXymbols 8051	Page Studio
Astrological[6]	PIXymbols 8052	Page Studio

[1] Alphabet, numbers, and symbols along with their ASCII codes.

[2] Within symbols.

[3] Unshifted.

[4] Display type and symbols.

[5] Symbols.

[6] Basic glyphs.

Symbol Subject	Font Name	Company
Bar Code§	Cape Cod	Dubl-Click
Borders§	Borders 1,2,3	Dubl-Click
Borders	El Paso	Dubl-Click
	Tijuana	Dubl-Click
Braille	PIXymbols 3000	Page Studio
Boxes	BulletsNstuff	EmDash
Bullets	BulletsNstuff	EmDash
Business-related Symbols	PIXymbols 5001	Page Studio
Calendar	PIXymbols 0101	Page Studio
Chess Symbols§	Odessa	Dubl-Click
Command Keys	PIXymbols 2115	Page Studio
Commercial Symbols	Universal News & Commercial Pi	Adobe
Conference Symbols	PIXymbols 6010	Page Studio
Dingbats	Carta	Adobe
Dingbats	ITC Zapf Dingbats	Adobe
Dingbats (decorative)	Ornaments	Adobe
Egyptian hieroglyphs§	Tanis	Devonian
Egyptian hieroglyphs§	MacTut/ProGlyph	Dubl-Click
Engineering Symbols§	Tempe	Dubl-Click
Forms Design Symbols	PIXymbols 3050	Page Studio
Fraction Components	Fractional	Devonian
Fractions, Avant Garde+	Afraction Plain	EmDash
	Afraction Bold	EmDash
Fractions, Courier+	Cfraction Plain	EmDash
	Cfraction Bold	EmDash
Fractions, Helvetica+	Hfraction Plain	EmDash
	Hfraction Bold	EmDash
Fractions, San Serif	PIXymbols 8022	Page Studio
Fractions, Serif	PIXymbols 8020	Page Studio
Fractions, Times+	Tfraction Plain	EmDash
	Tfraction Bold	EmDash
	Tfraction Bold Italic	EmDash
Greek	Universal Greek & Math Pi	Adobe
Highway Signs	PIXymbols 4010	Page Studio
Holidays	PIXymbols 0101	Page Studio

Symbol Subject	Font Name	Company
IBM Keys/Components	KeyCaps	Paperback
	PIXymbols 2008	Page Studio
	PIXymbols 2011	Page Studio
	PIXymbols 2013	Page Studio
Icons	Symbols Galore	Dubl-Click
Icons	Symbol City	Dubl-Click
Industry Symbols	PIXymbols 5002	Page Studio
Information Symbols	SInformation Signs	Studio 231
IPA	International Phonetic Association	Devonian
Letters in boxes/circles	PIXymbols 8010/12	Page Studio
Macintosh Keys	KeyCaps	Paperback
	PIXymbols 2011	Page Studio
	PIXymbols 2005	Page Studio
Macintosh Keys[1]	PIXymbols 2014	Page Studio
Macintosh Keys[2]	PIXymbols 2013	Page Studio
	PIXymbols 2113	Page Studio
	PIXymbols 2114	Page Studio
Macintosh Icons	PIXymbols 2000	Page Studio
Math Symbols	Universal Greek & Math Pi	Adobe
	Math Whiz	Dubl-Click
MICR Characters[3]	MICR	Adobe
Music Notation	Sonata	Adobe
Numbers Alphabets[4]	ASCII City	Dubl-Click
Numbers in boxes/circles	PIXymbols 8010/12	Page Studio
OCRs	Waterbury OCR	Dubl-Click
Office Symbols	PIXymbols 5001	Page Studio
PC extended character set	PIXymbols 2108/9	Page Studio

---

[1] European and French Canadian version.

[2] Thinline.

[3] Magnetic Ink Character Recognition.

[4] Alphabet, numbers, and symbols along with their ASCII codes.

Symbol Subject	Font Name	Company
Presentation Symbols	PIXymbols 6010	Page Studio
Religious Symbols§	Nazareth	Dubl-Click
Road Signs[1]	PIXymbols 4005	Page Studio
Runes§[2]	Rivendell	Devonian
Shipping	PIXymbols 5001	Page Studio
Signs & Symbols	SBusiness Signs One	Studio 231
State Map Symbols	PIXymbols 4010	Page Studio
Symbols	SBusiness Signs Two	Studio 231
	Symbols Galore	Dubl-Click
	Symbol City	Dubl-Click
Telephone Buttons	PIXymbols 8015	Page Studio
Thinline Keys		
Travel Information	PIXymbols 4018	Page Studio
	PIXymbols 4019	Page Studio
TV Listing Fonts	PIXymbols 8004/5	Page Studio
U.S. Maps Symbols	PIXymbols 4010	Page Studio
Weather Symbols	PIXymbols 0101	Page Studio

+ EmDash states that these fonts rely on *fonts that are already available in your printer. If you do not have Times, Courier, or Avant Garde, these fonts will not work on your printer.*

---

[1] International.

[2] Based on the runes and script of J.R.R. Tolkien.

Foreign Language & Symbol Font Companies

USA

Adobe® Systems, Inc.
1585 Charleston Road
Mountain View, CA 94039
(800) 83-FONTS / (415) 962-2100

Devonian International Software
P.O. Box 2351
Montclair, CA 91763
(714) 621-0973

Dubl-Click Software, Inc.
9316 Deering Avenue
Chatsworth, CA 91311
(818) 700-9525

EmDash
P.O. Box 8526
Northfield, IL 60093
(312) 441-6699

Page Studio Graphics
3175 N. Price Road #1050
Chandler, AZ 85224
(602) 839-2763

Paperback Software
2830 Ninth Street
Berkeley, CA 94710
(415) 644-2166

Studio 231
231 Bedford Avenue
Bellmore, NY 11710
(516) 785-4422

UK

Adobe UK Ltd.,
Minex House,
55a High St.,
Wimbledon,
London, SW19 5BA
081 944 1298 TEL

Kuma Computers Ltd.,
12 Horseshoe Park,
Pangbourne,
Berks RG8 7JW
0734 844335 TEL

Kuma Computers Ltd.,
12 Horseshoe Park,
Pangbourne,
Berks RG8 7JW
0734 844335 TEL

FontWorks UK Ltd
65-69 East Rd,
London N1 6AH
071 490 5390 TEL

Kuma Computers Ltd.,
12 Horseshoe Park,
Pangbourne,
Berks RG8 7JW
0734 844335 TEL

Paperback UK Ltd.,
The Widford Old Rectory,
London Rd,
Chelmsford,
Essex CM2 8TE
0245 265017 TEL

Type Technologies Ltd.,
Euston House,
81-103 Euston St.,
London NW1 2ET
071 387 5666 TEL

8 Index

Note: Font prefixes such as Adobe, CG, ITC, S, and VGC were not taken into consideration for alphabetization.